G000270561

WARTIME WANDERERS

WARTIME
Wanderers

A FOOTBALL TEAM AT WAR

Tim Purcell and Mike Gething

MAINSTREAM
PUBLISHING

EDINBURGH AND LONDON

Dedicated to the 'Wartime Wanderers'
themselves and their surviving relatives

Copyright © Tim Purcell and Mike Gething 1996

All rights reserved

The moral right of the authors has been asserted

First published in Great Britain in 1996 by
MAINSTREAM PUBLISHING COMPANY (EDINBURGH) LTD
7 Albany Street
Edinburgh EH1 3UG

ISBN 1 85158 913 9

No part of this book may be reproduced or transmitted in any form or by
any means without written permission from the publisher, except by a
reviewer who wishes to quote brief passages in connection with a review
written for insertion in a magazine, newspaper or broadcast

A catalogue record for this book is available from the British Library

Typeset in Sabon
Printed and bound in Great Britain by Butler and Tanner Ltd, Frome

Nat Lofthouse, O.B.E.

Burnden Park, Manchester Road, Bolton
Telephone: 0204 389200

To sum up in a few short sentences just how proud I am to be writing this foreword is a very difficult challenge. These men whose remarkable wartime experiences are told in these pages were my boyhood idols. As a schoolboy supporter I watched in awe from the terraces of Burnden Park as they were brought together for their football talent and made Bolton Wanderers a First Division force to be reckoned with.

All truly great teams possess an unbreakable unity which gives them the power to overcome their opposition whatever the circumstances. The Wartime Wanderers team spirit took them to great heights on the football field and transferred onto the battlefield when their country's need was greater.

In following their captain Harry Goslin's call to volunteer for military service en masse a glorious chapter in the history of football and war was opened. I was fortunate enough to be able to play alongside many of them after they returned from overseas, yet they never talked about the horrors that they had witnessed. It is testimony to their modesty that the full story has only now been brought to light for the rest of us to marvel at.

I was privileged to know these men and honoured to be a team mate to them. This is their story, I am delighted that the world will now know what I have known for so long – that they were true heroes. I am proud to say that I was their friend.

Nat Lofthouse
President
Bolton Wanderers Football Club
August 1996

ACKNOWLEDGEMENTS

Firstly we would like to thank the *Bolton Evening News* and their entire staff for their invaluable assistance and support, and for enabling us to have unrestricted access to their archival material. In particular we would like to thank the MD, John Waters; Editor in Chief, Andrew Smith; Librarian, Christine Bell; and photographer, Richard Rollon.

Also we wish to thank Allan Rogerson, Honorary President of the Royal Artillery Association (Bolton Branch), for providing us with much useful information, access to the Bolton Artillery museum, copies of war diaries and the Regimental history book, and also for donating several previously unpublished photographs, including several which are reproduced in this book with the kind permission of former Captain Ben Rees. We must also thank John Purcell for providing us with copies of his Regiment's war diary covering aspects of the war in the Middle East, accounts of the Dunkirk retreat and some original army newspapers published in Iraq.

We would like to acknowledge the support of the Bolton Wanderers Football Club, in particular Simon Marland, the club historian, who also enabled us to have access to the Trophy Room at Burnden Park.

Finally, in no particular order of preference, we would like to thank the following for their support and patience while we were researching and writing this book: Graham Lamdon for his patience, Sarah Gittins for exceptional PA services, Roger Samuels for co-writing the screenplay, Martin Darvill for his vision that is transforming Liscombe Park into a centre for creativity, Ed Sturmer for his percuniary assistance, and Florise Purcell for her full support and encouragement always.

AUTHORS' NOTE

This is a true story. Every incident in this book actually happened. Of 35 full-time Bolton Wanderers staff and players at the outbreak of the Second World War 32 volunteered for military or police service. The first 15 players who voluntarily joined the Territorial Army, and to whom we refer in the book as the 'Wartime Wanderers', were:

George Caterall,	Ernie Forrest,	Albert Geldard,
Harry Goslin,	Charlie Hanks,	Stan Hanson,
Donny Howe,	Jack Hurst,	Billy Ithell,
Sid Jones,	John 'Jack' Roberts,	Tommy Sinclair,
Val Thompson,	Ray Westwood,	and Danny Winter

During the course of our research we compiled many hours of taped conversations with the relatives, friends and comrades of the 'Wartime Wanderers', but only two of the surviving players. It is these collective personal memories that make up the bulk of the book, corroborated where possible with the articles that appeared primarily in the *Bolton Evening News*, together with private letters, notes and diary entries that were kindly passed to us. At times there were discrepancies, on dates and places, but these we put down to the passage of time. However, there was one tragic incident that was reported to us in graphic detail by a veteran of the 53rd Bolton Artillery that received scant mention in the media of the day. Even before the outbreak of hostilities the War Office intervened to sanitise the press. For the duration of the war the country was to be subjected to censorship and propaganda.

We therefore commit to print the recollections of Fanny Westwood, Alan Westwood, May Hanson, Margaret Foweraker, Jack Hurst, Jack Roberts, Jimmy Gittens, Eileen Greenhalgh, Sandra Hawarden, Bill

Killan, Billy Ainscow, Cliff Spence, Joyce Forrest, Alan Forrest, Nat Lofthouse and the many others who kindly helped us in our endeavours to preserve their memoirs, 'lest they forget'.

ONE

In the L.S. Lowry painting entitled 'Going To The Match', huddled figures in cloth caps, mufflers and clogs are seen walking towards a football ground in the north of England. The scene is set against an industrial backdrop of smoking mill chimneys and terraced housing, giving it the dark and foreboding atmosphere of industrial town life in the 1930s. Lowry used the streets surrounding Burnden Park, the home of the Bolton Wanderers Football Club, as the model for his painting. In doing so he captured the essence of this particular Lancashire town in the years between the two world wars.

In 1938 the dark satanic mills were still very much a feature of Bolton life. Although the boom years of the nineteenth century were over, many Boltonians remained employees of the town's textile and manufacturing industries. The mills, factories and bleach works were full of men and women for whom everyday life was a combination of long hours and hard manual labour. Leisure time was in short supply, many holidays were unpaid and virtually no disposable income was available to the working-class family. Because of these prevailing conditions the town and its people were intrinsically linked, each assuming the character and identity of the other. Bolton inhabitants were not exposed to many outside influences. Foreign travel for the masses was unheard of. Many of the townsfolk only learnt of the outside world through the pages of the *Bolton Evening News*. While the mass communication industry was burgeoning the wireless broadcasts from the BBC and the newsreel footage shown in the local cinemas served only to broaden their horizons with a distinctly nationalistic bias. So with only one in five of the town's population boasting a radio licence the majority were content to live their lives reacting to stimuli from their immediate environment.

Entertainment then, as now, was all about escaping from reality for a few hours each week. By 1938 there were three hundred pubs, thirty cinemas, numerous theatres, music halls and dance emporiums in the Bolton area. Add to this the two hundred churches and chapels and one has an idea of how the people filled their leisure time. During 1937 and 1938 a huge study of urban life was undertaken by the anthropologist Tom Harrison, under the name *Mass Observation*. Considered to be the largest detailed study of its kind carried out this century it focused on Bolton for its subject matter. Observers spent two years in the town recording everyday life in minute detail; *Mass Observation* concluded: 'On the whole people care about their homes and their few personal dreams (security, a holiday weekend at orientalised Blackpool, a fortune on the pools) and nothing else matters much except the progress made by the town's football club whose stadium draws each Saturday more people than go into the pubs or churches.' Bolton Wanderers Football Club provided the town with the one kind of mass entertainment that combined the ideas of escapism and hope, while also providing an outlet for public displays of civic pride. 'Going To The Match' was an important part of Bolton life.

Like the town itself the football club has tradition and stability as a large part of its character. The club was formed as the Christ Church Football Club by the church schoolmaster, Thomas Ogden, in 1874. Reluctant to accede to the vicar's request to attend the meetings that were being held in the church school the club began a three-year search for suitable alternative premises, constantly moving from one headquarters to another until finally settling at Pikes Lane and adopting as their permanent title the epithet this restlessness had earned them. Thus the Bolton Wanderers officially came into existence in 1877, and the club was to be one of the founder members of the Football League in 1888. Seven years later the club moved to Burnden Park to begin a residency that was to last more than a century. As had been predicted the opening of this 'modern' stadium created a wealth of new jobs, and for one keen 18-year-old, Charles Foweraker, who was initially employed as a checker, it was to be the start of a fifty-year association.

In 1915 when the secretary-manager, Tom Mather, volunteered to serve in World War I Charles Foweraker was invited to take over his post for the duration of the conflict. Having successfully led the club through the war years he was persuaded to take up the position on a permanent basis in 1919, with an annual salary of £400. Despite having no practical experience of the game he had an innate understanding of players and how to motivate them. They in turn had a great respect for this man they revered as a Victorian patriarch. Never one to be seen improperly dressed, even at home, Foweraker made the three-piece suit with the gold fob watch dangling from the waistcoat his trademark. A bowler hat completed the ensemble when he stepped outside. This combination of high self-esteem and powers of man management contributed to the tremendous success of the side he was able to build in the 1920s, a team that established the club's highest-ever League position and an unequalled record of three FA Cup wins during a single decade. Foweraker's other eccentricity was his reluctance to move with the times. As his daughter recalls, their household never owned a telephone, even though this was rapidly becoming an essential tool of modern business. If the club needed to contact Foweraker urgently a call was put in to the next door neighbour who would despatch a messenger with the relevant piece of information, a strange idiosyncrasy considering Charles Foweraker was one of the first football managers to see the sport as a commercial business, setting a record transfer fee of £10,000 for a player sold to Arsenal as part of an overall fiscal strategy.

The great team of the 1920s inevitably went into decline as its star players aged. In 1933 the club was relegated to Division Two. However, Foweraker had already begun to rebuild the playing staff with a combination of astute transfers into the club and the development of young up-and-coming talent. A well deserved promotion to Division One was achieved in 1935 and by 1938 Bolton Wanderers was once again a formidable team with many quality big-name players, an inspirational captain in Harry Goslin, and the luxury of being able to field one of football's greatest stars in their forward line, Ray Westwood.

The 14th of April 1912 was a notable date in more ways than one. It was the day the *Titanic* sank after striking an iceberg in the Atlantic Ocean on her maiden voyage, and it was also the birthday of Ray W. Westwood. Ray's life was to prove as dramatic as the date of his birth. By his late teens he was already a star of the Bolton side, and was well on his way to becoming one of the first footballers to develop a celebrity status outside the game. Charles Foweraker had brought Westwood to Bolton from the Midlands amateur club Brierley Hill in 1928. The record books show that Ray went on to score 144 goals from his inside left position for Bolton Wanderers in 330 appearances. In itself this is a remarkable achievement, but it tells less than half the story. Ray Westwood was a charismatic performer. His game was stylish, fast and skilful. His was the name that drew the crowds to Burnden Park in the 1930s. He was their hero, a player coveted by all the other first division teams, yet unavailable to any of them, at any price. Chelsea was one club that tried unsuccessfully to sign him for £12,000, which would then have been the world record for a footballer's signature.

In the 1990s if you mention Bolton Wanderers in conversation the one name that springs to everyone's mind is that of Nat Lofthouse. If you say the words Bolton Wanderers to Nat Lofthouse the inevitable smile will be followed by the words 'Ray Westwood'. Nat was a Bolton schoolboy in the late 1930s and shared the town's obsession with its football club. In particular Nat remembers shinning up the drainpipes at Burnden Park to catch a glimpse of his boyhood hero: 'He was an idol of mine. A brilliant player, who knew he was a good player, but wasn't big-headed. Over ten, fifteen, twenty yards he was electric. He mesmerised me as a boy, and I wanted to be like him.' Nat Lofthouse recalls one incident which clearly illustrates the level of passionate feeling among the population of Bolton that Ray Westwood's name could generate: 'As a youngster I was sitting in the Odeon Cinema in Bolton when a printed message appeared on the screen. "Ray Westwood will definitely play at Burnden Park tomorrow." There was such a bloody cheer, and even as a kid I realised what Ray Westwood meant to the people of Bolton.'

As an England international Westwood was able to use his reputation to attract sponsorship deals, a rare luxury for any sportsman in the 1930s. It was after his debut with the national team that he was approached by Brylcreem to model for their hair products on posters and printed advertisements. The immaculately groomed Westwood hairstyle with its razor-sharp centre parting was perfect for the Brylcreem image, and the manufacturers were quick to realise the powerful influence such an international footballer would have on the male population. Ray's dapper appearance and celebrity took him into the glamorous social circles of the entertainment world. Bolton's many theatres and music halls attracted big-name performers to the town and Westwood could be seen sharing a laugh, and a pint of ale, with the likes of Jack Hylton and George Formby. But it should be noted that this elevated position did not bring with it the fortunes associated with the game today. Footballers' earnings were limited to a maximum wage level, plus win bonuses, that was unanimously applied to all players. Even the Brylcreem campaign was not a money spinner for Westwood, as he was paid a mere five shillings (25 pence) for the use of his likeness on the advertising hoardings.

But Bolton Wanderers were far from a one-man team. Expertly guided off the field by Charles Foweraker they were blessed with the on-field leadership of Harry Goslin. Goslin was a natural captain, quick thinking and calm under pressure; he led by example. Signed as a youngster from the Nottingham club Boots Athletic for a donation of £25 in 1930, Harry Goslin made his debut with the Bolton Wanderers first team that same year. Always one to spot potential in the young, Charles Foweraker was quick to make Harry a regular member of the professional squad. Goslin was a tall, athletic, ramrod-straight man with piercing blue eyes, whose physical presence combined with his pleasant but firm personality made him the ideal choice for club captain, a position he assumed in 1936. Under his astute leadership the club's fortunes improved and by 1939 Bolton Wanderers was once more in the ascendancy. As a measure of Goslin's sense of responsibility, even as he was still aspiring to the peak of a football career, he was already preparing himself for life after his playing days were over. With a wife and two young sons to support Harry had opened a sports shop in Bolton that was already beginning to prosper through his inevitable association with a winning team.

Charles Foweraker had two other stalwarts in the team of the 1930s. Big Jack Atkinson had been signed from the County Durham side Washington Colliery in 1931. Although Jack's signature came without a price Bolton did make several generous donations to the Colliery club's funds. Atkinson was a giant of a centre-half, around whom the entire defence would mould itself. He possessed a no-nonsense attitude on the field that made him the ideal 'minder' for the club's more skilful players. Any opposing defender who chose to stop Ray Westwood by foul means would soon have Jack Atkinson chasing after them to mete out instant retribution. In contrast to these extrovert displays of almost naked aggression on the pitch, away from the ground Jack was the archetypal strong, silent type not given to outbursts of emotion. He was married to a petite yet very demonstrative lady. It was a constant source of amusement to the other players to find the diminutive Mrs Atkinson storming into their changing-room after a match or a training session to make sure her errant husband was on his way home, and not taking a short-cut via the nearest hostelry.

George Taylor, like Nat Lofthouse, was a dedicated one-club man. Having joined as an amateur in 1925 he was to serve the Bolton Wanderers as a player, coach and scout for over fifty years. Together with Goslin, Westwood and Atkinson he contributed to a combined total of 1,100 appearances in the 1930s before historic events intervened to alter destiny. But in the second half of that decade it was this quartet that Charles Foweraker used as the foundation for the team he was building.

New young talent was brought in to strengthen the side. Stan Hanson, a goalkeeper from Liverpool, made his debut in 1936 at the age of 20, and would eventually stay with the club for two decades. Stan's father was Norwegian, and as such he had registered the surname on the birth certificates of all four sons as 'Hansen'. Only when the boys went to school did their teachers insist on the anglicised spelling, Hanson. Harry Hubbick, a mine worker from Jarrow, was signed from Blyth Spartans in 1937 and became the Wanderers' regular left full-back. Welshman John Roberts was another 20-year-old who made his first League appearance with the club in 1938. Also establishing themselves were Donny Howe, Albert Geldard, Jack Hurst and last, but by no means least, Ernie Forrest.

Although he had won a cap for representing the Durham County English Schoolboy Eleven, Ernie Forrest did not see a football career ahead of him. Instead, upon leaving school he undertook an apprenticeship as a cabinet maker. But it was his performance as an amateur player that drew the attention of the scouts and he was signed to Bolton Wanderers as an 18-and-a-half-year-old apprentice in early 1938. Despite making only five professional appearances at Burnden Park before the outbreak of war, such was Ernie's impact on the team that he would be fondly remembered by all who came in contact with him. Long before the likes of George Best or Paul Gascoigne provided fodder for the tabloid press Ernie Forrest was performing antics that would enthral the crowds and his fellow players alike. He was a clown, and together with Ray Westwood a mad gambler, who would quite literally bet on drops of rain running down a window pane. Whenever a throw-in went their way Ernie would sprint to the side to take it, just for the opportunity to chat with the crowd and ask which horse had won the 3.30 at Haydock. Nat Lofthouse admiringly recalled Forrest's enthusiasm:

> What a character; there was only one Ernie Forrest. You couldn't think of any other player before or since like Ernie. He was remarkably, unbelievably fit. Bloody good player too. The crowd used to love him, and encourage him. He used to do all these antics, such as backflips when he put a good cross

in, and the crowd used to clap. The players used to clap. He was
the life and soul of the team. He lived as if he didn't have a care
in the world. I've never seen a happier guy. Harry Goslin would
let him go so far before bringing him in to line, but anything that
was good for the team was fine by Harry, and Ernie Forrest was
good for the team.

By 1939 the younger players had still managed to amass around
three hundred appearances between them and it was clear that Charles
Foweraker had built a strong team for Bolton's faithful supporters to
cheer. His values of team spirit, loyalty and hard work were being
passed on to the players by Harry Goslin, and they responded to this
guidance by becoming one of the best sides to represent the town in
the club's history.

It is apparent that the priority for Charles Foweraker was to
discover talented footballers from the ranks of amateur and school
sides whom he could sign at an early age and then mould into his ideal
player. Castle Hill School in Bolton had recently produced one of the
great England centre-forwards of all time, Tommy Lawton, and now
another pupil at this school, who also happened to be a fanatical
follower of Bolton Wanderers, was destined to set the world alight
with his own footballing exploits. Nat Lofthouse was from working-
class Bolton stock. His father, Richard, was a coalbagger who had to
keep a wife and four sons on a weekly wage of two pounds ten
shillings. Richard was not a great football enthusiast, and what with
his work, his allotment and his family commitments he didn't have a
great deal of spare time in which to oversee the progress of young Nat.
Naturally he would show an interest in his son's development but it
was to be a family friend, Bert Cole, who was to be Nat's mentor. Bert
had first seen Nat play for the school side when he was just eleven
years old. Nat had joined Castle Hill straight from primary school at
the age of ten, and by the time he was twelve he was selected to play
for the Bolton Schools team. After one memorable match against the
Bury Schools, in which Nat scored a remarkable seven goals, Bert Cole
rewarded him with the gift of a new bicycle.

When Nat was not playing football he would take every
opportunity to go down to Burnden Park to watch how the
professionals played the game. Football in the 1930s was still very
much a working man's spectator sport, and was priced accordingly.
The schoolboy Nat would have paid threepence to stand on the
railway embankment at the end of the ground, sixpence to stand on

the paddock along the touchline, and the princely sum of one shilling and threepence for a seat in the stands. From these vantage points Nat Lofthouse observed the skills and formations of the game, he marvelled at the unity between the players and the crowd that had paid to support them. To a young fan there were lessons to be learnt about the qualities and values of football in Bolton: 'What struck me was that when I went to watch Bolton Wanderers, the team seemed to play for one another. The crowd always seemed to be for them, and for one another. I think this is what got me used to Bolton people. Bolton people liked honest guys, they liked people who tried. If a player was putting it on then they didn't want to know. That made a big impression on me and I always had a good relationship with the crowd in later years.'

As the 14-year-old Nat Lofthouse was enjoying his football the rest of the adult population of Bolton was steeling itself in preparation for an altogether different contest: 1938/39 was the last full season of professional football before the outbreak of World War II. The season had been heralded by the futile hopes of Prime Minister Neville Chamberlain's 'peace in our times' speech, yet as the winter months passed by it became apparent that full-scale war was inevitable. All around the town Bolton people could see signs of an official campaign to prepare them for conflict. As early as September 1938, just as the football season was getting under way, a large consignment of gas masks arrived in the town. Within a matter of days all the townsfolk were fitted with a mask and told to familiarise themselves, and their children, with its use. Vast quantities of sandbags were already being stored at key locations. Even by the time of those inaugural matches it was estimated that Bolton had stockpiled some half a million sandbags, with volunteers working feverishly to increase this sum daily. By October the *Bolton Evening News* was publishing details of the newly built municipal air-raid shelters in the town centre, and advising people to memorise their locations in case of an emergency. The obvious presumption that any future conflict would feature air-raids on a significant scale was also helping to change the physical appearance of the town centre. In readiness for the anticipated blackouts kerb stones and street-lamp pillars were being painted white. Supplies of uniforms and specialist equipment to be used by the Air Raid Precautions (ARP) volunteers were constantly arriving.

In January 1939 the government's message to the people of Britain was that they had an official duty to assist in making the country ready for a state of war. The 25th of this month saw the distribution throughout all of Great Britain and Northern Ireland of the National Service Handbook. This publication provided information on the various occupations open to the public in such vital services as the ARP, the police and the Women's Land Army. Some 90,000 copies were distributed to households in the Bolton area alone, ensuring that the message would reach one in every two of the population.

While the country was physically still at peace, psychologically it was already at war, and the burning issue for the man in the street was how to prepare himself for training. The government of the day was wrestling with the alternative merits of compulsory National Service (conscription) and a voluntary call to arms via the Territorial Army. The government realised that each system had benefits to the national cause: conscription ensured that a full-time militia could be developed quickly and trained to its maximum potential expediently; the development of the Territorial Army on the other hand would train men on a part-time basis while still leaving them available for work. The two systems attracted both support and criticism from the working man. In early April 1939 the *Bolton Evening News* featured a debate on its letters page on the pros and cons of conscription versus the voluntary system of enlistment. Arguments for a compulsory National Service were centred around the fact that war was imminent and therefore there was a need for rapid preparation. One letter writer expressly pointed out the fact that the political situation had changed so swiftly over the recent weeks that the country was now committed to sending an expeditionary force abroad. The regular army at this time was small, especially when compared to that of Germany, and it was unrealistic to believe that the Territorial Army could be made ready for active service in just a few weeks, or even months. Clearly a full-time training programme would better prepare Britain for war. It would also enable the government to reconsider the upkeep of reserved occupations. Many women felt willing and able to take on the manual work in the Bolton mills and factories should the need arise due to the calling up of the male workforce, and conscription would ensure that this could be done in a controlled manner.

Another view strongly held at the time among those Bolton people who were in favour of conscription was the fact that if compulsory National Service was implemented it would drastically reduce the numbers of unemployed in the locale. However, perhaps an even more poignant argument in support of this system came from those who still harboured vivid memories of the First World War. Conscription had only been introduced in 1916 when the large numbers of casualties suffered made it necessary to boost the ranks of the armed forces. Many of the survivors from that era firmly believed that the army of soldiers lost in that conflict could well have been saved by better training. A counter argument was that conscription would take men away from the workplaces permanently and that such a massive surge away from the shop floor would leave industry irretrievably weakened. The government must therefore be urged to promote the Territorial Army as a viable alternative to create a full-time militia. There was also the very valid moral argument in favour of a voluntary call-up within Britain's internationally respected democratic framework. Many people felt that to force citizens to serve was taking away the liberty that every Englishman holds dear.

One letter to the *Bolton Evening News* (4 April 1939) summed up the feelings of so many: 'Sir, when a Briton takes up arms voluntarily his whole heart and soul are in the business. He fights hard, laughs at suffering, welcomes danger, all because his freedom is threatened. Take away that freedom by making him a conscript and you take away his chief reason for fighting. He becomes a mercenary, dissatisfied, fighting from fear of what his country might do to him, not of what a foe might do to his country.' Although this view was widely shared among the indigenous population it was unfortunately not reflected in the level of recruitment. Therefore, in a bid to increase the size of the Territorial Army the government began offering incentives to companies who were prepared to give their employees time off for the necessary military training. While many employers accepted the offer the resultant rise in the number of volunteers was often insignificant. A substantial element of the commercial community refused even to contemplate the option as they held the view that allowing Territorials to train during work time would result in an economically disastrous drop in productivity.

As the German menace increased in Europe the British government was desperately aware of the need to speed up its own preparations for war. A realisation grew that this half-hearted response to the call to arms may be due in part to the government's failure to capture the public's imagination with a vigorous 'propaganda' policy against the aggressor. Instead, ministers decided to promote the image of the Territorial Army itself. Although the Territorials may have been perceived as a reserve force, they were in fact the nation's heroes because they were all volunteers. Among the various organisations employed to promote this concept was the Football Association, which commanded the attention of the bulk of Britain's male population. In that same month of April, 1939, the Football Association sent a circular to all its members regarding the example to be set to the youth of the country. The FA asked the football clubs to take a patriotic stance and encourage their members to enlist in the Territorial Army or other National Service organisation. Charles Foweraker read this memo in his office at Burnden Park with keen interest. As a great patriot Foweraker felt that he should make the Bolton Wanderers Football Club a guiding light in the moves to prepare the town of Bolton for war.

TWO

Shortly before 3 p.m. on 8 April, Easter Saturday 1939, the massed band and drums of the 5th Loyal Battalion marched and counter-marched across the pitch at Burnden Park. A light rain that morning had taken the bone out of the ground, but done nothing to dampen the spirits of the fans who packed the stands and terraces to capacity for this home match against Sunderland. As they cheered in anticipation they were unaware that a microphone had been placed before the Centre Stand. Only when the band came to attention and the players, neatly attired in their blue training suits, lined up beside them did the crowd begin to feel the sense of occasion.

For the board of directors at Burnden the ongoing debate on whether National Service should be compulsory or voluntary had culminated in a unanimously endorsed resolution to support the government's Territorial Army recruitment drive. Football grounds throughout the country were being asked to promote the call to arms. With radio in its infancy and television purely experimental this was the most effective way of reaching the majority of the male population. But from what was heard of the experience at Blackpool on Good Friday and elsewhere throughout the weekend, that at Bolton was to prove the most successful in the country.

As the Bolton captain, Harry Goslin, stepped up to the tiny microphone many doubted whether this fragile apparatus would be man enough to deliver the goods. Unhesitatingly Harry began to speak, only occasionally glancing at the notes he had scribbled on a scrap of paper moments before. Used to taking command on the field of play Harry rapidly claimed authority, his voice booming out across the ground to penetrate every nook and cranny. The crowd fell silent. Some 23,000 beings were transfixed, by the man and the moment: 'We are facing a national emergency. But this danger can be met, if everybody keeps a cool head, and knows what to do,' he began. 'This is something you can't leave to the other fellow, everybody has a share to do.' Having outlined what was expected of those in attendance, including the women, who could, and would, volunteer for auxiliary services – nursing, driving ambulances and the like – Harry relinquished the microphone to the visiting captain who wished the appeal success. With just minutes to go before the kick-off Sir William Edge, a former Member of Parliament for Bolton and President of the club, came to the fore, flanked by co-director and city mayor Alderman Cyril Entwhistle. His speech was to be uncharacteristically brief, but poignant: 'I want to ask you one question. Are we in Bolton, standing here on this ground, prepared as the Germans or the Italians to stand up for the security of our children?' A tumultuous 'Aye,' erupted from the crowd, and shook the very rafters of the stadium. Picking up on this euphoria the military band struck up a familiar strain. Never before had the National Anthem been sung with such gusto.

That evening the *Bolton Evening News* carried the ominous banner headline 'Italian Troops Occupy Albanian Capital'. Quite incongruously the double column photograph beneath this further evidence of the threat to peace in Europe was not of the fires and looting in Tirana, the Albanian capital, but of a smiling Harry Hubbick and his new bride, captioned 'Wanderer Married'. Such was the esteem in which the local football team was held that even the growing menace pervading the continent from Mussolini's pact with Hitler could not mar this happy event, although Harry's decision to take to the pitch with his team in preference to attending his own reception may not have made this the happiest day in Mrs Hubbick's life.

The match had only just finished as this late edition was going to press so even if the reporters at the ground had been privy to the post-mortem taking place in the changing-room they would not have made it into print. Unlike any other match day, the players were not enthusing about their 2–1 victory over Sunderland, they were continuing the national debate. It was obvious from Harry Goslin's positive delivery that his mind was already set. Westwood was not so sure. He had only returned to the side that day after a spate of injuries, and at 27 was still some way from reaching his peak. Interrupting his career to join the army, even the part-time Territorials, could have profound and far-reaching consequences. The ever exuberant Ernie Forrest had joined the club as an apprentice at 18 and a half. Now, two years later, he had still only played five League games, insufficient to elevate him to full-time professional status. Exchanging the cleaning of football boots for the spit and polish of army beetle crushers could permanently block that promotion. It was because of these thoughts that he probably shared Stan Hanson's ideal that the situation was not as grave as the media and the government would have them believe. Others, like Jack Hurst, would follow their captain without question. Big Jack Atkinson, who had been known to slide into the deep recesses of the communal bath to escape the wrath of his spouse, would not shirk his responsibility in the face of this threat to national security and freedom. The decision process for some of the remainder was far more fundamental. The War Office had stressed that there could be no guarantees, on compulsory call-up, that men would be drafted to the units of their choice. There was a very real possibility that Albert Geldard would be conscripted to his home unit in Glasgow; others would be posted to regiments in Cardiff, Swansea or Sunderland. But by far the most decisive factor was their loyalty to each other, born out of years of shared glories and hardships. As a team of long standing they had played hard together, both on and off the pitch. Perhaps as a logical extension of this bonding they vowed to support each other, and take their indomitable team spirit from the playing field to the battlefield.

The following Monday afternoon Sergeant Bill Killan, a long-serving career soldier, was on duty at the Territorial Army recruitment office, a former shop on Bradshawgate, when the entire Bolton Wanderers first team, led by their captain Harry Goslin, came to join the 53rd Field Regiment of the Bolton Artillery. Ray Westwood had gone home after the match on Saturday but had said nothing to Fanny. His father, Sam, must have had some idea of Ray's intention when he returned to Bolton a day ahead of schedule to take this first opportunity since Harry's speech to put the words into action. Ray paid no heed to his father's advice not to put pen to paper.

The atmosphere in the Westwood household at Brierley Hill in the Black Country was to remain strained for several days after Ray had recklessly condemned his future to uncertainty. Sam, whose own fighting he restricted to the amateur boxing ring as an occasional prize fighter, was convinced Ray had committed professional suicide. Ray's fiancée, Fanny, who had moved in with the Westwoods after her parents had tragically died some years previously, was unable to heal the rift. Instead she chose to adopt the same stoic pose as the mother, as they meticulously prepared Ray's kit for the following weekend's away match at Aston Villa, a match that was to be the Trotters' final victory in the last full season in peacetime.

There was a macabre air of foreboding at Burnden Park when the shutters came down for the close season. In a bid to dispel the gloom that the gathering war clouds were casting over their world Ray and his team-mates threw themselves into the social whirl. Despite the seven years' difference in their ages Ray Westwood and Ernie Forrest were developing a close friendship that was to last a lifetime, not least because of Ernie's ready wit. Even when Ernie turned up for a soirée sporting a brand new and expensive camel hair coat to mimic Ray's flamboyance, it was met with good humour. It was still Ray, with his celebrity status, who was the toast of the dance halls, and the vaunted companion of entertainers and notorieties. He would frequently be seen in the company of Jack Hylton, whose big band headlined at the Palais, where the Bolton Wanderers were offered free admission because their presence always attracted more customers, and the more upmarket Empress, at the time owned by Harry Goslin's in-laws. On one memorable evening his friend of many years, George Formby, presented him with a signed ukulele as a mark of respect for his sacrifice in volunteering to fight for his country, an act that Formby dearly wanted to emulate but one that the War Office declined, preferring instead to book him as an entertainer.

The international tension that was to build throughout that summer of 1939 was very much in evidence in Norway when the Bolton Wanderers arrived for their brief tour at the end of May. But even the ominous threat of an imminent Nazi invasion could not mar Stan's excitement at playing his first foreign tournament in his father's homeland. They had always been close, but had never had the opportunity to travel back to his father's roots together. Now, being able to capture something of the background atmosphere that had moulded the character that Stan both loved and admired would help strengthen the bond even more.

It was to be a short-lived euphoria. When Stan and his compatriots returned from what within a year would be enemy-occupied territory the consequences of their own actions in volunteering for the armed services were now inescapable. As their own military training intensified the national recruitment drive continued to gather momentum, with each month seeing the records shattered. On 12 July, only a day after the Nazi collaborators had told the 400,000 Jews in Hungary to 'starve or get out', the British government announced an additional £80 million war budget. That same day the *Daily Mirror* launched a campaign to get Winston Churchill appointed to the Cabinet. Large display advertisements appeared in the regional press throughout the British Isles lauding his virtues as 'the only public man whose political forecasts have been and are consistently and devastatingly accurate'. Daily demonstrations were now being given by firefighters and the civil defence on everything from blackout preparations, to dealing with magnesium electron bombs. Explicit instructions were also imparted to enable everyone to extinguish fire bombs, fit gas masks and to be able to practise decontamination after those inevitable gas attacks. The letter that Charles Foweraker had received from the FA way back in January 1939 calling on his team's support of a 'National Fitness and Air Raid Precaution Publicity Drive', suddenly took on a more ominous meaning.

It was against this backdrop of war despondency that 34 officers and 530 other ranks, including 17 Bolton Wanderers players attached to the 53rd Field Regiment, assembled at Trinity Street railway station for the journey to summer training camp in Trawsfynnydd, North Wales. An advance party had already left by road with the fight vehicles. The trunks and bundles of equipment that had been laid out on the floor of the artillery drill hall in Silverwell Street were now taken by the package party onto a second train that also carried the guns, including eight howitzers and eight eighteen-pounders. Nearly one thousand shells were to be fired in that fortnight.

This first major training exercise for the boys from Burnden Park was to be marred by a tragic accident. In the sanitised version of the incident released by the War Office at the time only one casualty, Gunner Boardman, was to remain hospitalised, with chest and stomach injuries, a fact that seriously conflicts with the description of events related by Cliff Spence, who was not merely an eyewitness, but one of the victims. Although the unit had arrived at the small station of Trawsfynnydd, 14 miles inland from Harlech, during daylight hours, it was to be dusk before sufficient transport could be mustered to relay them to the camp. The country's real state of preparedness now became evident. While the war machine was believed to be stepping up a gear in a bid to meet the might of the Germans, much of the equipment available to the Territorial Army had been mothballed since the Great War of 1914-18. The trucks that now arrived to pick up the remaining troops were already veteran. Cliff managed to push his way onto an already overcrowded vehicle, and leant over to give Ray Westwood a hand up. But Ray was distracted by a shout from Ernie Forrest, and declined Cliff's assistance, instead opting to scramble to join his team-mate aboard the following lorry. It was dark when they pulled out of the station forecourt. In readiness for the coming hostilities the vehicles were required to travel with blackout lights, providing only the narrowest beam of light to illuminate the treacherous mountain roads. In the back the men and equipment were being mercilessly thrown together. Gone was the barrack room banter, replaced by an almost unearthly quiet, broken only by the deep throb of the antiquated engine and the relentless grinding of gears as the driver fought to manoeuvre the vehicle through the tortuous terrain. As if in slow motion the truck suddenly slid into the cliff face and ricocheted across the path of the following vehicle before colliding with a tree and plummeting into the gully. The fragile lorry disintegrated as it crashed through the scrub, tossing out its cargo of men and equipment like so much worthless flotsam. Cliff's last recollection was of floating through the air with other soldiers and their kit tumbling over him. When he regained consciousness he learnt that eleven men had been killed and fifteen injured.

The reported success of the two weeks of training would always be tainted in the minds of the men who were under oath to remain silent. Even the families knew little of what had happened. Both Fanny and May Braithwaite (Stan Hanson's girlfriend) were aware that there had been an accident, but the details remained vague, and would eventually fade into the mists of time. For the readers of the *Bolton Evening News* on 24 July it was the record set by the 53rd Field Regiment that was of paramount importance. For the first time at Trawsfynnydd 16 guns were in action with four observation posts manned simultaneously, a feat that had not been achieved since the days of the First World War.

For much of the fortnight, however, the weather was poor. There were days when low cloud obscured the range, preventing them from firing until well into the afternoon. There were also complaints about the food, which was excused by the messing arrangements that had previously only been required to cater for a battery of 78, not a full regiment of several hundred. Outside the camp there was little provision for amusement. The nearest village was some five miles distant, and although it boasted a public house and a cinema, the seating capacity of the latter was limited to just 40 people. For the Wanderers, who were celebrities in their home town, this was a rude introduction to the harsh realities of military life.

Perhaps more than most of them Harry Goslin adapted to these alien conditions, and brought to his new-found role those same

qualities of leadership that had placed him at the helm at Burnden
Park for many years. By the time they returned to Bolton to commence
training for the new football season he had already been promoted to
Sergeant. Not that he would allow this perceived 'officer' status to
affect his relationship with the team. He would still indulge them in
their revelry, especially Ernie Forrest who seemed to find humour in
every situation, and a ready audience in Stan Hanson and the others.
Only Jack Hurst tended to remain aloof from their shenanigans, but
with good cause. His wife, Betty, had given birth to a boy some
months earlier, and the child had not stopped crying. What the doctors
put down to colic, Jack believed was something far more serious. He
felt for the infant, and his cries of pain. He also knew that it was fairly
evident that the coming conflict would see them separated. His long-
standing friendship with Harry Goslin was to be reinforced when they
pledged to protect each other's family in the event of their absence
even though, for the moment, there was to be a brief respite from
thoughts of war, as they reported to Burnden Park.

Nationally moves were afoot to change the 'charging' rule, and in a
bid to improve the game for spectators it had been proposed, and
adopted, that players should carry numbers on their backs, something
many may have seen as being too akin to the army's method of
individual recognition. It could even have been construed that the
sport itself was now being dictated more by the political events.
Certainly the usual rash of transfers had been seriously curtailed in this
general mood of uncertainty. As for the Wanderers, they were to see
some changes that were specifically designed to improve their skills on
the pitch rather than the battlefield. For instance, a tarmac tennis court
had been laid at their training ground to enable a game of ball control
to be played across the net; in addition, the directors and training staff
of Bolton Wanderers had debated whether or not to introduce a
revolutionary treatment pioneered by Wolverhampton Wanderers,
whereby players were injected with monkey gland fluid to enhance
their performance. The dissenters at Burnden Park won the day,

As the players turned out for their first training session of the
1939/40 season such innovations would have played second fiddle to
the international scene that was becoming ever more complicated. No
doubt in response to this global crisis the Football Association had
removed Rule 33 from the Rule Book, which stated that 'No player
serving in His Majesty's Forces could be registered as a professional
footballer'. But there were conflicting accounts appearing in the
dailies, and the players may even have been tempted to breathe a sigh

of relief as they read 'Storm Clouds Over Danzig Disappear', only to find that another dark and threatening bank had appeared over Yugoslavia. What was more, the pending conflict was spreading to engulf the entire globe. The peace talks with Japan that had been postponed on 17 July now seemed unlikely to ever be rescheduled as 50,000 hostile Japanese, presumably mobilised by the military, took to the streets of Tokyo to demonstrate against Britain. Only the veteran Japanese statesman Yukio Ozaki was prepared to stand up in parliament and openly oppose the all-powerful Imperial Army with scant regard for his own life.

In an article appearing in the Associated Press at the beginning of August the 80 year-old Mr Ozaki stated his demand for Japan's neutrality while the government itself was embroiled in the question of joining the Italo-German military alliance. Radical quarters of the army were unequivocally in favour of joining. The navy, the business interests, and the Liberals were not. Ozaki's arguments had a basis in historic fact. By remaining neutral during the Great War Japan's wealth had more than tripled. In the coming conflict, he claimed, 'in all probability there would be a recurrence of much greater intensity'. If they were to stay out of the coming war, he could foresee a scenario that would peacefully achieve their ambitions, granting Japan economic control not just of the Far East, but the entire world. 'The European powers,' he continued, 'would have no course other than to come to Japan for materials and supplies. Almost immediately Japan would restore to her coffers more than she has spent on the China campaign,' a stagnating military adventure that was ultimately to prove disastrous. As he continued to reflect upon prevailing opinion, he could not have known just how prophetic his words would be: 'Granting that the two Powers – Britain and America – cannot afford to send their entire naval forces to the Far East, yet Japan would have to pay dearly for annihilating their fleets, perhaps even at the cost of fatally crippling her own. If neutrality is impossible the next best thing would be for Japan to side with the democracies,' Mr Ozaki declared.

Just four days later, with petrol rationing already announced, the British army embarked upon its largest-ever manoeuvres. Double-strength battalions of the Territorial Army took up temporary residence at camps dotted about the country. This vast mass of khaki-clad men and petrol-driven fighting machines concentrated on various home fronts, ready for action. Officers from the allied armies of France and the Benelux countries were invited to observe the development of these all-important exercises. The British artillery put their anti-aircraft defences to the test during a mock attack on Liverpool by French bombers, and the sales of Andersen bomb shelters soared. In this climate of war readiness the Prime Minister was obliged to warn the Japanese, 'We have a fleet, but prefer discussion to threats.'

Throughout August the situation continued to deteriorate. On 7 August Herr Forster, the Nazi leader in the supposedly free city of Danzig, had forcefully claimed that , 'Danzig would soon, very soon, return to the Reich.' In Hong Kong British soldiers were obliged to face off the Japanese, whose own naval fleet had already implemented a blockade of Canton. One thousand troops of His Majesty's Armed Forces lined the mainland border with China. Open conflict now seemed inevitable.

Never before had professional football been resumed under such tense circumstances. Even though there had been doubts and misgivings during the crisis of September 1938, when the German threat to Czechoslovakia saw France mobilise her own troops along the Maginot Line, Chamberlain had rescued the situation through diplomacy. Yet, before he was able to brandish that now famous piece of paper, there were many footballers who expected their very next game to be played behind the lines somewhere in Europe. If there had been doubts about Britain's willingness to fight when Germany finally made its unhindered push into Czechoslovakia in March 1939, now was the time for them to be dispelled. In those last two days before the opening matches there was every reason to believe that the fixtures would be suspended, despite the assurances of the Football League authorities that the programme for Saturday 26 August would proceed 'unless the international situation takes a more serious turn'.

The signing of the Russo-German pact a few days before, which had resulted in the Anglo-French military missions breaking off negotiations and leaving Moscow, was swiftly followed by Poland closing its border with Danzig, now firmly in the grip of the Nazi 'Head of State', Herr Forster. Flanked by articles depicting Germany's complete readiness for war, and the published instructions from the British consulates for their resident citizens to leave Germany, an official of the Football Association issued his own written statement: 'We are carrying on as usual, unless we receive instructions from the authorities to cancel matches.' A declaration that was quickly endorsed by the Football League headquarters' even more direct release to the press: 'Saturday's matches will take place, unless there is war. In which case it is unlikely that the Government will allow big gatherings of people.' For Bolton Wanderers this meant a trip south to commence the new season where they had finished the last, at Stamford Bridge, London, the home ground of Chelsea FC.

As the team made their final preparations for this inaugural game the daily media revelations were increasingly alarming as the country was 'confronted with the imminence of war'. The IRA, who saw this growing conflict with Germany as an opportunity for securing a military ally for their own cause, detonated a huge bomb in Coventry city centre, devastating buildings, destroying buses and trams, and causing many injuries and serious loss of life. It was reported that immediately after the explosion pitiful screams and cries were heard in all directions. Even in the wake of this terrorist attack on home ground Britons were being urged to leave France. Many anxious to fly home aboard the fleet of special planes commissioned by Imperial Airways were seeing their wishes hampered by bad weather. Fog had closed in on Croydon, London's only passenger airport.

Hitler's perceived diplomatic triumph in signing the pact with Stalin was attracting rising anger from the Japanese, whose leading commercial daily, the *Shugai Shogyo* accused Germany of being, 'dead to moral sense'. With the publication of the provisions of the German-Soviet Non-Aggression Treaty there were those in the media and the government who began seriously to question the advisability of concluding a military alliance between Japan and Germany. Buoyed by these assertions President Roosevelt made a last-minute appeal to the main protagonists, while simultaneous efforts were being launched by the Russian Foreign Minister, V.M. Molotov, through their Ambassador in Poland, moves that were met with the closure of the Dutch-German frontier. The French Prime Minister, Edouard Daladier, prepared to launch a 'sacred union' appeal, similar to that broadcast on the eve of the Great War, summoning the total support of the nation, and Mussolini called another 500,000 men to arms.

Right up to departure time on that Saturday, 26 August, the Bolton Wanderers' manager, Charles Foweraker, was ready to cancel all arrangements for the visit in the event of a sudden call on the country's Territorial forces. This would have taken into armed service most of the team chosen to play in the match. To demonstrate his readiness to face any emergency Charles Foweraker deputised a second team to travel to London and fill the boots of the artillery men in his squad. Such was the gravity of the situation that the Football Association had already rescinded their rule preventing a soldier in the regular forces being a registered professional footballer. The day of the Chelsea

Ray Westwood in the Bolton Wanderers
strip that was in fashion when he joined
the club in 1930.

Donny Howe sports the kit introduced in the
mid 1930s which for the first time boasted
the club badge modelled on the town crest.

Goalkeeper Stan Hanson poses for a photographic article that appeared in the *Topical Times* in August 1938, showing him at work, rest and play . . . Stan was an all-round sportsman who, when not playing football, enjoyed cricket, tennis and even American baseball, representing a semi-pro team from Liverpool.

Stan Hanson in action against Middlesbrough on 7 January 1939. Note the sand that had been placed in the goalmouth to soak up the rainwater and prevent a quagmire from forming.

WILLS'S CIGARETTES

R. W. WESTWOOD
(BOLTON WANDERERS)

THIS SURFACE IS ADHESIVE. ASK YOUR
TOBACCONIST FOR THE ATTRACTIVE
ALBUM (PRICE ONE PENNY) SPECIALLY
PREPARED TO HOLD THE COMPLETE SERIES

ASSOCIATION FOOTBALLERS

A SERIES OF 50

47

R. W. WESTWOOD
(*Bolton Wanderers*)

Although he had a trial with Aston
Villa, Raymond Westwood joined
Bolton Wanderers probably owing to
the fact that his uncle, David Stokes,
had played for the Lancashire club.
He signed on in 1930 soon after
leaving school and became a
professional at the age of seventeen.
Born at Brierley Hill, near Birmingham, Westwood first played at
outside-left for the Wanderers, but
as his physique developed he moved
into the inside position and became
prominent for his wonderful pace and
deadly shooting. He played for England for the first time in 1935, against
Scotland, Wales and Holland, and
he has now six caps to his credit.

W. D. & H. O. WILLS

MANUFACTURERS OF GOLD FLAKE, CAPSTAN,
WOODBINE AND STAR CIGARETTES

BRANCH OF THE IMPERIAL TOBACCO CO.
(OF GREAT BRITAIN & IRELAND) LTD.

Long before the sticker albums that are popular with children today, collectable cards were to be found in cigarette packets. This was one of a later series, when Ray Westwood had already won several international caps.

W. ROWLEY

BOLTON WANDERERS

In Exchange for **25**
of these REAL PHOTOS,
sent post paid and per-
fectly clean, a **Cabinet
Photo** of any one of the
series of either Foot-
ballers or Cricketers
will be sent free.
For **100** a
Large Real Photo of
any one of the League
Teams will be sent.

Address: "Photo,"
112 COMMERCIAL ST.
LONDON, E. 1.

Another collectable series . . . This time featuring Walter Rowley who joined the club in 1912 and was to remain with them for 38 years, as player, coach and manager.

An advertising flyer promoting Dolly Blue, a dye manufactured by William Edge & Sons. Sir William Edge was a former MP for Bolton, and Chairman of the Bolton Wanderers football club.

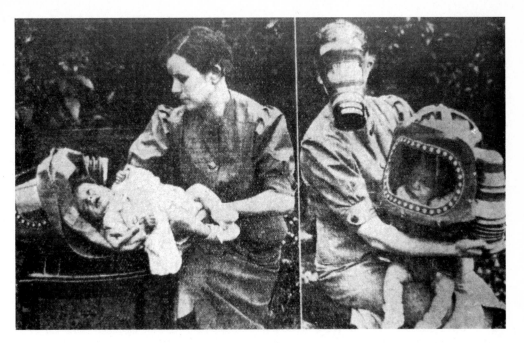

Although gas masks had been distributed as early as September 1938, this pictorial demonstration of the infant appliance did not appear in the *Bolton Evening News* until 15 August 1939.

This picture of Stan Hanson with his Norwegian father was another from the *Topical Times* feature that was published on 6 August 1938.

The Bolton Wanderers touring squad that visited Norway, the homeland of Stan Hanson's father, at the end of the season in May 1939. (*left to right*) back row: Harry Goslin, Jack Hurst, Stan Hanson, Jack Atkinson, Harry Hubbick, Jack Connor. Front row: Danny Winter, Donny Howe, Albert Geldard, Tommy Sinclair, George Hunt, Ray Westwood, Teddy Rothwell (Assistant Sec.)

The 'Wartime Wanderers' were invited to the Palace of Westminster by their local MP, John Haslam. The Mayor of Bolton and club director Cyril Entwhistle accompanied them and signed the photograph.

Officers at summer training camp, Trawsfynydd, Wales, July 1939. Third from the right in the front row is Captain R.W. Greenhalg, a career officer who, after his promotion following Dunkirk, was to be appointed CO of the 53rd Field Regiment, Bolton Artillery, a position he was to maintain for the entire duration of the war.

In the grounds of the disused Raikes Mill, Captain Greenhalg oversees the new recruits as they learn the art of open-air cooking.

TA Drill Hall, Silverwell Street, Bolton, where the 'Wartime Wanderers' were first billeted. The 'memorial' was erected the day they were shipped out.

Just a week after war was declared the Bolton Wanderers were back at Burnden Park but this time wearing the regimental strip. (*left to right*) back row: Danny Winter, Harry Goslin, Jimmy Ithell, Stan Hanson, George Catterall, Jack Hurst. Front row: Albert Geldard, Tommy Sinclair, Donny Howe, Jack Roberts, Val Thompson.

match a special committee had drafted a circular that was to be distributed to all clubs, in which it was stated, 'the release of militiamen to play football, or arrangements for the postponement of their training, will not be subject to any rigid and defined rules, but will depend upon "the exigencies of the service".' Even as this text was being put to bed Hitler was making his final demands for Danzig, the Polish Corridor, and an end to the Anglo-French pledge to Poland.

Under a fine summer sky the teams turned out before a crowd of 30,000. The Wanderers had all of the play, but most of the bad luck. Even though the fans were treated to some brilliant moves from Ray Westwood that brought the house down on more than one occasion, and a fine goal from Donny Howe five minutes before the interval, they were to suffer a 2–1 defeat. Having been subjected to this ignominious result the Wanderers were then obliged to fulfil another away fixture at Stoke City on Monday 28 August, even as feverish last-hour efforts were being made to avert war. While the government awaited Hitler's response to its latest note the teams took to the pitch. All the best play came in the first half, keeping the crowd on tenterhooks as the ball travelled rapidly from one goal to the other. The Bolton defence put up a gallant show, with Hubbick sticking like a leech to Stoke's star player, Stanley Matthews, severely restricting his effectiveness. In the event it was to be two chances well taken by Hunt and Rothwell that won the match for the Wanderers.

Despite their victory on this outing things did not augur well for the remainder of the season. A hastily convened meeting of the Football Association, the League and the War Office declared that no such general permission would be given for called-up players to be released for matches, even though it was expected that officers commanding individual units would accommodate such requests where possible. As the month of August drew to a close Britain's towns and cities became strangely quiet as 1.5 million children, labelled and clutching their few personal possessions and gas masks, were evacuated to safe areas in the country. Their parents had been told to send them to school with no more than spare clothing, toothbrush, comb and a handkerchief, and a bag of food for the day, but with little or no knowledge of where their offspring would be spending that first night away from home. The Coronation Chair was also taken by train to an unknown destination.

All the nations were hurrying forward with preparations for war. Germany cancelled their Tannenberg celebrations, commemorating Hindenburg's defeat of the Russians in 1914, as it moved more troops to the eastern border. Italy now had better than two million men under arms. Seeking refuge in the countryside, streams of civilians fled Paris, their belongings piled high on any transport they could muster. Their military mobilised more men and tanks along the German frontier. Pontoon bridges were cut and railroad bridges mined at strategic places across the Rhine. France's North African defences were put on a high state of alertness. Through their embassy German nationals were advised to leave London.

For the young Nat Lofthouse, playing football at Castle Hill School, the harsh realities of the situation had yet to sink in. His own father being too old for call-up, Nat had no immediate experience with which to relate. The football season had started and the only priority on his mind was blagging his way into Burnden Park Stadium for the Trotters' first home match on Saturday 2 September. What he was totally unaware of was the fact that the Trotters had also been watching him.

The board at Burnden Park must have been conscious of the grave situation their club was in. With their entire first team already committed to the army they would have no players, other than reserves, to represent the Wanderers during hostilities, and even these might soon be called up. Their survival would depend on attracting players below military age. Given Castle Hill School's reputation for having provided both Everton FC and the national side with one outstanding player in Tommy Lawton, perhaps it was not surprising that the football scouts had been present. Their attention may even have been drawn to Nat by his father's friend, Bert Cole. Bert had taken it upon himself to coach and encourage the young boy. Every Sunday morning he would take Nat and his brother Tom, who was in the same school team, to the local playing field where they would practise heading and shooting.

Nat probably also took scant heed of the first evacuees arriving in Bolton from London as his attention was still focused on the coming match, the first in the new season that he could actually get to see. He had heard that France had postponed all her professional games, but with no information to the contrary officials of the British Football Association were still confident that the fixtures for the coming weekend would be carried through. Even as late as Friday 1 September, as Nat and his fellow pupils were filing into their school hall for the annual prize-giving ceremony, the President of the Football League, Mr W.C. Cuff, announced that none of the following day's matches were to be cancelled. Individual clubs, however, were advised to keep their ears open for the wireless and their eyes open for the press, as the government would take any action necessary through these media.

The first inkling that Nat had of any interest in his footballing talent was when he took to the stage to receive a prize from the local mayor, Councillor Cyril Entwhistle. As a member of the board at Burnden Park he was authorised to ask Nat Lofthouse if he would like to play for the Trotters. If the answer was in the affirmative he would have to get himself down to the ground first thing Monday morning and report to the manager, Charles Foweraker. There was no hesitation. This was Nat's dream.

As Nat sprinted down Manchester Road that Saturday afternoon he chose to ignore the rumours that several players had already been called up in the wake of the Polish crisis. Shortly after dawn the previous day, without any declaration of war, Germany had unleashed her forces that had been concentrated for more than a week along the Polish frontier. Taken completely unaware, the Poles were to suffer horrendous losses as bombs rained down on their major cities, an operation launched on the back of Danzig's proclamation that the former free city was now part of the German Reich. Obligated to fulfil their pledge Britain, along with France, authorised the complete mobilisation of the army, navy and air force. The Press Association was able to reveal that a widened War Cabinet would, in all probability, include Mr Winston Churchill.

Nat's only thought as he shinned up the drainpipe for the last time to take his familiar spot on top of the Manchester Road Stand was of the imminent game. With the international scene overshadowing events the gate was not what it would have been under normal circumstances. As the visiting team, Portsmouth, kicked off towards the Great Lever End goal the attendance numbered fewer than 8,000. But much to the delight of Nat, his hero, Ray Westwood, was on the field and in fine form. The crowd rose as the Portsmouth defender, Morgan, deceived by a bouncing ball, failed to check a headlong rush by Wanderers' famous inside left. Westwood's terrific pace, which Nat longed to emulate, was giving Bolton the initiative. Attack after attack had the visitors pressed into their own half. When they were able to break free their forwards never showed the same clever combinations the Wanderers were serving up. By half-time the fans on the terraces and in the stands, now swollen to better than 12,000, were relishing their home team's aggressive tactics, which were to be rewarded with a 2–1 victory.

Nat was mesmerised as he witnessed the winning goal. A long kick up field by Hubbick was met by an opponent, only to fall to Donny Howe, who successfully baffled the keeper with a smart left-foot lob that sped over his head and into the top corner of the net. The following week Nat would be inside the ground with these players, signed as an apprentice for the only team he would ever play for, Bolton Wanderers.

THREE

Sunday 3 September 1939 was a warm 'Indian' summer's day in Bolton. As the people of the town settled down to breakfast the newspaper headlines and radio broadcasts announced Britain's latest ultimatum to the German government to withdraw from their occupation of Poland: 'Unless not later than 11.00 a.m. British Summer Time today, September 3rd, satisfactory assurances to the above effect have been given by the German Government and have been received by His Majesty's Government in London a state of war will exist between the two countries as from that hour.'

Bolton, indeed the whole nation, sat and waited for 11 a.m. to arrive. Bolton Wanderers supporters reading the sports pages of Sunday papers would have registered their team's home victory over Portsmouth. In the end some 13,000 of them had bothered to turn out to watch the game at Burnden Park despite the threat of an imminent declaration of war. They had witnessed some bright, well planned football and a win over the current FA Cup holders that could easily have been by a far greater margin. The Wanderers had won two of their first three games in the 1939/40 season and the first League tables published in those same Sunday editions saw them placed equal third in Division One. Charles Foweraker's team-building expertise was beginning to reap rewards, but the Burnden faithful were to be denied the talents of this newly settled team. Eleven a.m. arrived and no assurances from Germany had been forthcoming. At 11.15 a.m. Prime Minister Chamberlain broadcast his solemn message to the nation. Britain was now at war. The news was greeted with jingoistic enthusiasm in London where a crowd had gathered outside 10 Downing Street. When the Prime Minister left for Parliament a mass of cheering people thrust forward to praise his decision to fight. Tension had given way to great excitement and the people of Britain were steeling themselves for whatever the future would bring.

In Bolton itself 3 September had been an intense day of preparation. At the civic centre the continuous work of filling sandbags was going on apace fuelled by an almost perpetual stream of lorries. The Public Health Offices, Air Raid Precaution Centre and the town hall itself were all open, with officials engaged in supervising the operations in readiness for the coming emergency. The news of that momentous announcement by the Prime Minister had the effect of clearing the streets of pedestrians. Even the few cars that were to be seen were predominantly engaged on official business. Immediately after the broadcast volunteers began to congregate outside the town hall, eager to do their civic duty. For a short while a lengthy queue accumulated as the civil defence personnel were caught off guard by this sudden influx of willing manpower. Those that did stay home made strenuous efforts to protect their own houses with sandbags. People who had not treated the recently imposed lighting restrictions too seriously immediately set to work on the total blackout of their homes and businesses. Vehicles were hastily equipped with light-diminishing blinkers. Bolton was battening down its hatches in readiness for the expected aerial onslaught.

The formal declaration of war also meant rapid call-outs for the Territorial Army volunteers. A radio announcement from the BBC suggesting that all Territorials should report for duty to their local headquarters immediately was followed to the letter by one young Wanderers player. Albert Geldard was in his digs close to the Bolton town centre when he was shaken into activity by this authoritative broadcast. Without hesitation Geldard grabbed his uniform and his gas mask and ran as fast as he could to the Drill Hall in Silverwell Street to declare himself ready to serve his country. The hall was virtually deserted, except for one bemused sergeant who was amazed to see this keen young recruit standing before him. Geldard was told quite brusquely not to be so daft, there was nobody there and not likely to be until the evening, when he should return at 7.30 for the parade as usual.

Albert Geldard's enthusiasm would not have been shared by the older players, whose wives and families were to be deprived of a breadwinner, with a larger than average pay cheque. Nor by Ray Westwood, who would not let a day pass for the duration of his enlistment without letting someone know that, 'this was the worst decision I've ever made in my life'. Neither would it be shared by

Charles Foweraker whose fears for the decimation of his team were to be realised almost instantaneously.

Not the entire population of Bolton was to be totally absorbed in the international news that Sunday. For Nat Lofthouse this was merely the day before he reported to his beloved Bolton Wanderers to sign apprentice forms. Even as he walked excitedly down Manchester Road on the Monday morning he had not paused to consider what immediate effect the declaration of war would have on the club. He was therefore ill prepared for the scenes of chaos that confronted him as he turned on to the Burnden Park forecourt. Players and their families were gathered agitatedly outside the offices and club house, awaiting military transportation. Workmen busied themselves replacing the closed season shutters.

Football as a professional sport, in an organised league form, was over. The Football Association had decreed some months previously that the outbreak of war would cause the immediate suspension of League competition. In addition the Home Office restrictions placed on any large public gatherings were all-encompassing and in the months leading up to this conflict allocating clerical staff to the work necessary to amend legislation that would make football an exception had hardly been a priority. Charles Foweraker had arrived at Burnden Park that day with mixed feelings. He privately thought that football in some form would soon be permitted by the government, as it had been during the Great War. This did not alter the fact that his current crop of first-team players were being called upon to exchange the playing field for the battlefield. A board meeting was therefore called for the following evening to discuss the whole position in which the club now found itself. Not wishing to pre-empt any decisions they would make Foweraker, in an interview with a *Bolton Evening News* reporter over the weekend, had merely stated the obvious: 'We cannot continue to pay out players' wages with no money coming in.' He was also able to confirm that the first six of the fifteen players that had joined the 53rd (Bolton) Brigade of the Royal Artillery had received their calling-out papers, and the other nine would obviously follow quickly.

Ernie Forrest, along with George Catterall, Sid Jones, John (Jack) Roberts, Val Thompson and Charlie Hanks, was the first to be advised by the army to request that Bolton Wanderers FC send their National Health Insurance cards to London, and their unemployment cards to the local labour exchange, while they themselves were ordered to report to the Drill Hall with their civilian gas masks, and their Army

Book 3 in which their pay and service record would be entered. Failure to report would make them liable for prosecution. Charles Foweraker had also received a circular from the Football Association that morning requesting the names of all men at Burnden Park with qualifications as physical instructors, or masseurs. Given the nature of the club it was a foregone conclusion that all members of the Bolton Wanderers training staff could be classified under one heading or the other. The future looked more bleak by the minute.

As Nat Lofthouse walked slowly towards the player's entrance he saw several of the first team congregated in the tunnel. Curious as to what they were doing Nat hesitatingly approached his heroes, who up until that moment he had only ever viewed from afar. He was horrified to discover that they were all waiting to pick up their employment papers, which would effectively terminate their engagement with the club. Amid all this confusion Charles Foweraker still had his mind focused on the future of Bolton Wanderers. Spotting the nervous fourteen-year-old he gestured for Nat to come into his office. Despite the turmoil and the uncertainty occasioned by the day's tragic events Nat Lofthouse duly signed his apprentice forms as had been previously arranged. Walking away from the ground Nat reflected on the history he had seen unfolding around him. In the aftermath of such confusion Nat wondered what opportunities, if any, lay ahead of him in the world of professional football.

For Bolton Wanderers and all other existing professional teams the change of lifestyle was to be both rapid and drastic. In accordance with pre-war football policy the secretary of the league, Mr F. Howarth, calmly announced that football had been suspended and all club contracts with players were automatically cancelled. A suggestion by the players themselves that the League's Benevolent Fund, currently standing at £50,000, should be used to pay their wages was rejected out of hand by the League President Mr C.W. Cuff. It was, however, deemed possible that some of this fund could be used to support hardship suffered by players' dependants as a direct result of the war.

This issue of wages was already a delicate matter. Although all professionals effectively received the same salary, there were some anomalies associated with varying fees for home and away matches, which over the course of a full year would balance out. With three games already played some clubs had enjoyed two home fixtures, while others, including the Wanderers, had played only one. Therefore the difference in revenue generated served to create an imbalance in players' incomes for the first time in the game's history, a potential dispute that was to dissipate as the Bolton Wanderers Territorials found themselves in the regular army. Being among the first to respond to the call they were immediately billeted in Silverwell Street Drill Hall for an initial fourteen-day acclimatisation period. Late arrivals and new recruits had been allowed home as soon as the limited accommodation was taken up.

Even with his first team vastly depleted Charles Foweraker was hoping to get football matches staged at Burnden Park as soon as possible. All throughout that first two weeks of war the debates between the clubs, the Football League and the Football Association were gathering momentum. It was soon decided that friendly matches could be played subject to police approval. Charles Foweraker lost no time in gaining such assurances from Bolton's Chief Constable. With his players still billeted locally Foweraker appealed to the Commanding Officer, Lieutenant Colonel G. Bennet, for permission to field his first eleven for one last time. Bennet understood the importance of this match to the town and granted his consent for all the players to be made available to the Bolton Wanderers, on the condition that they wore the Regimental strip. To further endorse his support of the game Lieutenant Colonel Bennet also arranged for the Regimental band to play for the entertainment of the crowd, and it was further agreed that men in uniform would be admitted at half price.

The fact that the Bolton Wanderers first eleven were in uniform so quickly was a great source of pride to the local community. Back in April 1939 not all clubs in the country had lent their support to the Football Association's recommendation to promote the army recruitment drive. Manchester United's directors had been in total disagreement with the notion, declaring that it was a matter for each individual to decide. Consequently when war did arrive the Manchester United players had to rapidly find alternative ways to serve the nation, or be drafted. The *Bolton Evening News* previewed this first friendly match to be arranged in wartime between Bolton Wanderers and Manchester United at Burnden Park under the headline 'Wanderers Soldiers to Oppose United's Munitions Workers'.

Football's reappearance at Burnden Park was good news for the club's season ticket holders. As soon as the Football League had been suspended a debate arose about whether or not individuals who had purchased a season ticket should be reimbursed by the club which they had paid in advance to see. Ironically many of those season ticket holders had already joined the armed forces themselves and were therefore unable to attend the matches anyway. But for the Manchester United game there were one thousand season ticket holders who would be grateful of a match to see. It was decided that a season ticket would be valid for all friendly matches whether at home or away, until a final decision had been made about how to structure wartime football.

The Burnden Park crowd on 15 September was dominated by those in military uniform, and the few members of the public that were able to attend did so carrying their gas masks, a poignant reminder of the hostilities taking place overseas. The contest on the pitch was keenly fought, with both teams fielding close to full-strength line-ups. Despite a tendency by some players to take things easy the Wanderers started brightly and went into an early lead through Donny Howe after Ray Westwood had wrong-footed United's defence with a neat dummy. Harry Goslin missed a penalty later in the first half, but by half-time the crowd were cheering the players on, losing their cares and worries for the duration of the match. With the final whistle the game ended in an honourable 2–2 draw.

This outing was to win for the Wartime Wanderers the first of many mentions in the army dispatches, which would form part of their individual service records: 'Complete soccer entertainment by McKay, great-hearted show by Goslin, sound goalkeeping by Hanson, who played in odd boots. In fact a great show all round.' The *Bolton Evening News* on Monday commented that friendly matches would well be worth seeing if the standard of this opening game could be maintained. Furthermore, as an exercise in morale boosting the match was also a big success. Five thousand people had been thoroughly entertained on a sunny afternoon and were still able to be home before the 7.15 curfew that the town had introduced, but would not maintain. Encouraged by the smooth running of this game Charles Foweraker was able to organise another friendly fixture for the following Saturday against Liverpool at Anfield. This would be a final chance for the Bolton Wanderers first eleven to play together before their military service began in earnest.

A short leave followed the Manchester match, to allow the men to say their farewells to families and loved ones before returning to their unit, now relocated to a large disused mill in Raikes Park. This threw the Wanderers together with the ordinary menfolk of Bolton, who in normal times would be cheering them on from the terraces, now unified not only by a common desire for a different kind of victory, but also by the fact that they were to fight for that victory as members of a regiment bearing the town's name. One local man in particular was thrilled to stand side by side with the players in the ranks of the 53rd Field Regiment, Bolton Artillery. Billy Ainscow was a keen and talented amateur footballer from the Halliwell area of Bolton, who had played regularly for Bradshaw Football Club in what was known as the Sunday School League. At the time a great deal of organised recreational activity was centred around the church and social clubs, but the title 'Sunday School' was somewhat of a misnomer as it was in actuality an amateur league for adult players. Billy Ainscow was a mainstay of the Bradshaw team, which was one of the strongest in a league that was being regularly scoured by Bolton Wanderers on the look-out for newcomers to bring into the club. Right at the beginning of the season Bolton scouts had visited the Rigby Lane Ground where Bradshaw played and had focused their attention on the wiry Billy Ainscow. But before the club was able to make an official approach history had intervened to deny Billy his opportunity. Instead of taking to the field in the white and navy colours of Bolton Wanderers Billy was destined to line up with Harry Goslin and the team in the red and blue quarters of the Regimental strip.

Raikes Mill was a former textiles mill on the Burnden side of town barely a few hundred yards from the Wanderers' home ground. Billeting Territorial Army personnel in their home town at the outset served several purposes. It kept the men together and ready for immediate action without severing family ties completely. It also got them into the disciplines of army life while simultaneously providing an environment in which the men could bond into a strong cohesive unit. Raikes Mill itself was a tall imposing building inside which there were a series of landings arranged around a central atrium, connected by a system of steel ladders. The rooms off these landings on the upper floors were where the troops slept. In his entire army career Billy Ainscow was to be hospitalised only once, and that was to be in a Bolton hospital.

After a day's training the men, who were virtually all locals, were neither allowed to venture into the town of an evening or even go home, as they needed to grow accustomed to a segregated army life. However, in order to provide some recreation a mess and bar had been installed for the enlisted men on one of the upper floors. Westwood, Forrest and Hanson would invariably be the first ones to the bar every evening. After one particularly heavy session imbibing with his new-found buddies Billy Ainscow staggered off to his sleeping quarters having downed a couple of beers too many. Waking up in the middle of the night Billy set off in search of the toilet. Unfortunately he missed his turning in the complete darkness and walked straight over the edge of the landing, severely spraining both ankles as he came to rest on the concrete floor, with a crash and a scream that woke the several hundred men encamped in the mill. A ten-day hospital stint followed before Billy was able to return to the Regiment.

Meanwhile the Bolton Wanderers directors had agreed to maintain a policy that the club had originally introduced during the First World War, namely the awarding of benefit payments to players as a form of compensation to cover the war period. Harry Goslin and Ray Westwood were granted benefits for long service that would be paid whether they played for the club again or not. The club certainly acknowledged that with both players in the army it was highly unlikely they would be able to play in the Bolton colours again until the hostilities were over. However, as they had both already completed nine years' service at Burnden Park they qualified for loyalty payments. A special clause was written into their benefit agreements authorising any eligible payments to be made to their dependants should anything happen to them during the fighting. Two other long-serving players, Taylor and Hunt, also had benefit payments imminent. With the arrangements for Westwood and Goslin already ratified the Bolton Wanderers directors had in fact entered into a gentleman's agreement that undertook to count war service as playing service in those cases where the bulk of the benefit period had already been served. A great deal of the credit for this arrangement must go to Charles Foweraker who continued to have the mutual interests of the club and its players as an inseparable priority. With the suspension of the Football League all payments to Foweraker himself had also ceased, yet he was prepared to work without remuneration in order to maintain football at Burnden Park for the people of Bolton to enjoy.

Charles Foweraker had been a part of a successful Football League reorganisation during the First World War and fervently believed in a similar system being implemented in 1939. During the week following the Manchester United friendly encouraging news had emerged from the Football Association's headquarters. In response to a government request that recreation and entertainment should continue as far as possible, they had consulted with Home Office officials. It was announced that, subject to several conditions, the Football Association would give its full support to friendly and competition football matches confined to local and district groups of clubs, on Saturdays and Public Holidays during the war. The conditions were that in evacuation areas the number of spectators would be limited to 8,000, or half the capacity of the ground, whichever was less, and that these should be evenly distributed throughout the stands and terraces. Admission would be by advance ticket only, and under no circumstances could football interfere with National Service activities. Here was a framework within which a League programme could be organised and Charles Foweraker was the first to stand up and declare the Bolton Wanderers ready to compete.

When Billy Ainscow arrived back at Raikes Mill the word was already out of an imminent relocation to Alnmouth in Northumberland for intensive gunnery training of the volunteer forces. The local soldiers billeted at the mill were allowed one more leave before moving out. For Ray Westwood, with his family in the west Midlands and another football match on the Saturday, this was not going to be possible. Instead of Ray going home to Brierley Hill his fiancée, Fanny, arranged to travel to Bolton to visit him at Raikes Mill. Arriving at the stark premises on an overcast afternoon Fanny's first impression was of a dark Dickensian prison, an image that reflected Ray's own concept of army life as enforced incarceration. The vision of these foreboding barracks did little to prepare Fanny for the appearance of Ray Westwood the soldier. Gone were the elegant looks and the slick hairstyle. These had been replaced by ill-fitting Regimental khaki and the severe styling of the army barber. As Ray felt the clippers slide up the nape of his neck all semblance of his former self dissipated. For the duration he would remain unkempt, slipping into obscurity, hoping he would not be recognised. In the army Ray wished only to be just another anonymous number, not the sporting celebrity of civilian life. When it was time for Fanny to depart the couple said a fond farewell, with Fanny vowing to travel the length and breadth of the country whenever there was a chance to spend even just a few hours together during Ray's restricted leave periods, knowing full well that throughout the course of Ray's intensive training these may be few and far between.

Stan Hanson used his leave to marry his fiancée of many years. They had met in Liverpool when they were both in their late teens. Even when he signed to Bolton Stan would commute in order to be with May as much as possible. They were a perfect, and inseparable couple. As Stan's position in the team became more secure he finally decided to move into digs with Donny Howe and Ernie Forrest in the Farnworth district of Bolton. At the beginning of the 1939/40 football season May had also moved to the town. Arrangements for their

wedding were already under way when war was declared. The hastily
organised church ceremony was followed by a reception at the
Empress Dance Hall attended by virtually the entire team of Bolton
Wanderers, in what was to be their last great shindig. But for Stan and
May there was to be no honeymoon.

As ordered the 53rd Field Regiment of the Royal Artillery moved to
Alnmouth at the end of September. For all of the men a new army life
was now beginning in earnest and so it was with some trepidation that
they made the journey north. Despite the loss of so many players
Charles Foweraker persuaded the board of directors at Bolton
Wanderers to keep the club open for whatever matches they could
muster. Another friendly game, this time against Blackpool, had been
organised for 30 September and new methods of team building were
being developed by the astute Foweraker. Football authorities had
been quick to sanction a 'guesting' system whereby available players
could turn out for any nearby team on a one-off basis. In order to
facilitate this arrangement at short notice the players had been offered
a match by match pay deal.

For the game against Blackpool Foweraker had selected from three
main sources. Firstly there were a small number of players from the
first-team selection list who had chosen to serve their country from the
home front. Harry Hubbick, the Geordie mineworker, had opted to
resume his career down the pits and was to remain in the Bolton area
for most of the war. In addition Jack Atkinson, who was eventually to
transfer into the army and serve in the Italian campaign, joined George
Hunt in volunteering for the police force. The more mature trainer/
player George Taylor became an army fitness instructor. These four
were to become regulars in the Bolton Wanderers War League games.
Secondly, Foweraker looked to those players under military age who
could now be given a chance in the senior side. Finally, he resorted to
the guesting system to supplement his team selection.

On the day before the Blackpool match the *Bolton Evening News*
had reported on the difficulties in raising a team for the game. It stated
that after a week of juggling with names, seeking other clubs'
permission to borrow this and that player, and trying to find work
during the weekdays for those stranded professionals whose services
they required on the Saturday, Foweraker believed he had put together
a viable side. Throughout those harrowing seven days there had been
setbacks and disappointments. Selected teams were named, then
withdrawn for one reason or another. The only certainty was that
there would be guests in the side. The two who finally took to the

pitch were both Bolton men at home on leave: Richardson was currently signed to New Brighton, and Tom Butler to Middlesbrough.

Action in the North West Division of the War Regional League proper kicked off on 21 October 1939, just seven weeks after the suspension of the Football League programme. Bolton Wanderers were away to Burnley on the opening day of the new competition and came away with a point from their 1–1 draw, their only goal a penalty scored by the new club captain, Harry Hubbick. A crowd of 3,000 had witnessed the game and generated some much-needed revenue for both clubs. This match also marked the rise to prominence of Charles Foweraker's latest protégé. Walter Sidebottom was a product of the club's youth policy and had made his debut for Bolton Wanderers in a 3–0 home victory over Birmingham City in February 1939. Despite the fact that this had been his only League appearance for the Wanderers to date Foweraker knew that Sidebottom was up to the challenge of first-team football now that the Territorials had all been called up to battle.

Meanwhile, in Alnmouth, the 53rd Field Regiment was being put through its paces as the harsh realities of army life were being driven home to Ray Westwood and the other professional footballers of Bolton by their new mentor, Regimental Sergeant Major Andrew 'Ranji' Hawarden, the nickname he had acquired because of his uncanny ability to mimic the spin action of the international cricketer Ranjit Singh. This was a fortuitous posting for Ray and the boys because Hawarden was first and foremost a footballer, having played professionally for the same Tranmere Rovers team that boasted the great Dixie Dean among its squad, and later on the books of Southend United. So it was hardly surprising that when Hawarden discovered that the entire Bolton Wanderers first team was amongst his latest batch of new recruits, he lost no time in organising a Regimental team. In his quest 'Ranji' Hawarden found a ready ally in Harry Goslin, who strongly believed that his 'Wartime Wanderers' should have the means to maintain and enhance their unique team spirit. He felt it essential not just for their morale but for the morale of the entire regiment that they should sustain their involvement in football as much as possible throughout the war. As Harry had envisaged the founding of the team served to unite the men of the 53rd in the most positive way. The troops gave their full support to the games that were initially played between regiments and training camps, and very soon the 'Wartime Wanderers' became known as a formidable force in army football.

This was a period that was to become known as the phoney war. No one could say with any degree of certainty whether or not the Territorials would ever be called upon for active service. Indeed it was the opinion of many pundits that the war would be over by Christmas and that normal life would resume soon thereafter. Even in Harry Goslin's own mind he was still very much the Bolton Wanderers captain rather than a Sergeant gunner in the Royal Artillery. With this belief at the forefront of his thoughts Harry contacted Charles Foweraker. Despite no longer being officially employed by the Bolton Wanderers he wanted the club's permission and Foweraker's blessing for his Regimental team to continue playing. Of the original 15 players to sign up, 13 were now stationed at Alnmouth. Only Jones and Hanks had been left in Bolton as they were under the age for active military service, which was then set at 20. Ernie Forrest had just scraped in. As a matter of course Harry Goslin was given the permission by his former manager, Charles Foweraker, to play the 13 as a team wherever and whenever matches could be arranged. Not only was this granted willingly but the players were also informed that they could assist any professional club requiring their services as guests. As a further sporting concession the Bolton Wanderers had been allowed to take their football boots, which officially belonged to the club, with them on army duty so they would be ready to play at all times.

In October 1939 Harry Goslin arranged for a match to take place in front of the paying public between the Wartime Wanderers and Jack Atkinson's former team, Washington Colliery, with whom the club had maintained ties. In fact the Wanderers' scouts had always made regular visits to the north-east, where colliery teams were well represented in the amateur football leagues. Indeed it was while watching one of these matches that they had discovered Harry Hubbick. Following hard on the heels of the Washington game came a challenge from Ashington, who could not resist the temptation of inviting some First Division stars to their Portland Park ground. Although in both matches Goslin's team was to play under the name of their battery, the football-mad Geordies of the area were well aware that the representative team of the 53rd Field Regiment Royal Artillery was in fact the First Division professional side, Bolton Wanderers, a fact they could not help alluding to in their match programme which read: 'No visiting team since Aston Villa played here on January 11th 1924 has included so many players of national and international repute as that which the Portland Park patrons are privileged to watch today.'

The glowing reports continued as the Regiment took on a Newcastle

United side at St James's Park. A local newspaper columnist reviewing the Army XI's 1–0 victory described the action in complimentary terms: 'Bolton Wanderers – beg pardon, an Army XI – yesterday showed a Newcastle United team how to play football at St James's Park. The Army team certainly had the best of the exchanges and a 1–0 win scarcely did them justice. There was Ray Westwood to "fiddle" the home defence into bother, there was quick response from his colleagues and hey presto! the Newcastle defence was turned inside out. The goal that decided the issue, a Westwood 25 yard shot, came in the 40th minute.' The Wanderers excellent display did not go unnoticed by the Newcastle United officials either, who acted quickly in seeking permission to make use of the Bolton players as guests. During the winter months of 1939/40 both Donny Howe and Ray Westwood were invited to turn out for the Magpies at St James's Park.

For Ray Westwood this was seen as a last chance for him to play to a crowd, and he wanted to put on a show they would never forget. Westwood did not like the discipline of army life and was already becoming totally disenchanted. He would have followed Harry Goslin anywhere, but the curtailing of his individuality was hitting him harder than any of the others. St James's Park was one of the classic football stadiums and Ray wanted to perform in style. The match was Newcastle United versus York City on 28 October 1939. Westwood and Howe were in rampant mood. In front of 5,300 people Ray Westwood scored a hat-trick from the inside left position and created several more scoring opportunities for centre-forward Howe who bettered Ray's own tally by scoring five times. Newcastle ran out 9–2 winners and the two Wartime Wanderers returned triumphant to their camp having provided eight of the goals for their adopted side. This was to be Ray Westwood's one and only game for a Football League side under the guesting system and he had left his paying public in a blaze of glory.

Between 11 November and 2 December three England international matches were played in quick succession. The last of these was between England and Scotland and brought a further honour to Harry Goslin who, at the age of 32, was selected to play for his country for the first time. Although not officially recognised as full international matches these wartime games were by no means second-rate. England's line-up included the now legendary Stanley Matthews, Joe Mercer, Raich Carter and Tommy Lawton. Goslin was in the finest company on the field and contributed to England's 2–1 victory in front of the maximum allowed capacity of fifteen thousand.

Just as the artillerymen were settling into their section training at Alnmouth the situation in Europe was growing more threatening for Britain. Germany was gathering for an offensive towards the west and preparations for action at home were speeded up. As a consequence the 53rd Field Regiment was relocated south to Swindon during the bitterly cold January of 1940. The Wanderers were to remain in Swindon until the second week of April. It was a period of intense gunnery training with the ominous threat of being posted into heavy action overseas constantly hanging over them. Weather conditions did not help matters. All of the water supplies at the army camp were frozen up for a two-week period in February. Each day at 6 a.m. the troops had to race across snow-covered fields to the nearest public toilets for their morning wash and shave, a race the Wanderers would invariably win. The heavy snows also brought down telephone and power lines, severing essential communications. In addition to their other duties the soldiers now found themselves seconded to the Post Office to erect telegraph poles and run cables in order to restore these vital services.

Despite the hardships they were enduring, football remained in the minds of Goslin and his men and they continued to seek out opportunities to play. In the Football League table following the declaration of war Swindon Town were positioned bottom of the Third Division South, having taken only one point from their opening three games. During the first season of wartime regional football, however, Swindon played twenty-eight games and were defeated on only eight occasions. Their close proximity to the army training camps had enabled them to tap into the guesting system to their maximum advantage and avail themselves of the top-quality professional players encamped on their doorstep. In the few months that the 53rd were stationed in the town no fewer than six Bolton Wanderers men turned out in Swindon colours. As an added treat for the local residents in March 1940 the Wartime Wanderers also played a match against Swindon Town. Once again billed as an Army XI Harry Goslin and his team attracted 2,000 supporters to this friendly match. As the army only provided one kit, red and blue quartered shirts, the Swindon players were obliged to wear their second strip of all white to avoid a clash of colours. An entertaining game resulted in a 2–1 win for the Army team who thrilled the spectators by fielding a full-strength Bolton Wanderers team for the fixture.

While they might have put on an outward display of living their lives as normal, many of the men at the Swindon camps were naturally nervous about what the future would bring. The prospect of being pitched into battle for real was a sobering reminder of their mortality and some big decisions had to be taken. War weddings were becoming a regular feature of everyday life for Britain's armed forces. In peacetime Ray Westwood had been happy to keep his mind on football and enjoy the celebrity status that it gave him. Ray's fiancée Fanny had often wondered if she would ever get her man down the aisle, despite the fact that they had enjoyed a long courtship. Ray and Fanny had been born in the same street in Brierley Hill, and had grown up together as neighbours and school friends. Romance blossomed in the early stages of Ray's football career and Fanny had learnt to accept the lifestyle that his vocation brought them. Most of Ray's week would be spent in lodgings in Bolton; he would return to Brierley Hill on Saturday night after the match and travel back on Monday for training. In spite of this time apart the couple grew closer together, especially as Fanny had been living in the Westwood household since losing her parents in 1936. It seemed to Fanny that this arrangement would go on for ever, until the war focused Ray's mind on his deeper feelings.

Swindon was a demanding training camp which moulded the volunteers into a homogeneous fighting unit. Although he was still active in the Regimental matches Ray Westwood had begun to shun the limelight that he had enjoyed for so long. Ray did not elect to guest for Swindon Town, preferring instead to reorganise his priorities before being fatefully shipped abroad. When Fanny arrived home from work on Friday 16 February 1940 it turned out to be her lucky day. A telegram had arrived from Swindon: Ray was coming home on leave that weekend for the first time since his call out, and he wanted to get married immediately. In all their years of courtship Ray had never even bought Fanny an engagement ring but now he had decided to make a lifelong commitment to her. Of course this left Fanny and Ray's parents with some hasty preparations to make. On the Saturday they were due to place flowers on Fanny's mother's grave, as it was the anniversary of her death, but on this occasion when the family called into the florist and ordered wedding bouquets instead they were greeted with exclamations of surprise and joy. Brierley Hill locals knew Ray well and were delighted at the news. The villagers all rallied round, and despite rationing Fanny was able to obtain the flowers, ham and tongue for the reception, and even to book the local church and vicar for the ceremony.

On the Saturday evening Fanny was making the final alterations to her future mother-in-law's own wedding dress that she was to be wearing when they heard Ray's footsteps crunching across the frosted ground behind the house. Fanny panicked. She could not be seen in the wedding dress. As she hurriedly donned an overcoat there was silence. The footsteps could no longer be heard, and the expected turn of the door handle also failed to materialise. Fanny raced outside with Sam and stared into the pitch darkness. They could not have been mistaken. They had all heard the footsteps. Suddenly a muffled curse reached out to them from the back garden and the realisation of what had happened dawned on them. Ray had fallen into the hole his father had excavated for their bomb shelter.

With his pride bruised more than his body, Ray finally married Fanny at 9 a.m. on Sunday 18 February 1940 in the Brierley Hill church they had attended in their childhood. It was a small, private service, especially as so many were away in the service of their country. Even the best man was only a casual acquaintance, Ray's own brother having been unable to get leave. The reception that followed was similarly attended by neighbours and ageing relatives too old for the forces.

The army gave no concessions to romance either and that Tuesday Ray had to report back to Swindon. His return to camp was signalled by an increase in activity for the Regiment as it soon became apparent that they were to be shipped abroad. The situation in Europe had deteriorated to the point where British troops were now essential to the defence of France if the country were to prevent the seemingly unstoppable German offensive reaching English soil.

On 11 April 1940 a road party left Swindon for the Southampton docks.

FOUR

For Ernie Forrest and many of the others their embarkation from Southampton for Cherbourg was to be their first excursion to foreign soil. For the Regiment it was to be the start of another military adventure in the Bolton Artillery's long history, a history graphically depicted on the Regimental marching drum that accompanied them. This particular bass drum had been manufactured after the last war, when its predecessor was presumably destroyed, or lost. Now resplendent in vivid colour, proclaiming the scenes of past campaigns, it was to sound their advance into another embattled chapter.

This main body arrived in France on 19 April 1940, two days after the advance road party that had transported the guns and heavy vehicles. Harry Goslin and Albert Geldard had been flown in to the country as early as 10 February as members of a British army football team; because of the hostilities a prearranged international match against France had been cancelled. As a morale boost for the British Expeditionary Forces, some of whom had been stationed in Europe since the previous October, the War Office had decided to stage the football game in Paris as originally planned, although now it was to be against a French army side, half of whose players were called back from the Maginot Line to perform. On this outing it was to be a British victory before a raucous crowd of 30,000 predominantly uniformed spectators. By all accounts this may not have been too uncommon. Selection for the national army team during this period of 'phoney war' would have followed similar guidelines to those in peacetime, and the professional players chosen could have been transported to and from the match on the specific orders of their immediate CO, as happened in other theatres throughout the following six years.

With Germany's main invasion forces still engaged in a concentrated attack on the Scandinavian countries of Norway and Denmark, the small villages of Saint Denis and Saint Martin d'Anjou, just west of Le Mans, where the 53rd were now billeted, must have seemed far removed from the hostilities. Little wonder then that the Regimental team was able to participate in a number of friendly matches with their French hosts.

As the month of April drew to a close and Hitler's forces turned their attention towards the Low Countries, the Bolton regiment was redeployed north to Lille. By now Ray had won the accolade of scruffiest soldier in the army, a title he bore with pride. In direct contrast to those heady days when he was the toast of the town he felt that by becoming anonymous he would cease to exist as a personality. On armistice he would quietly slip back into his crown and resume his reign at Burnden Park. Unfortunately his fame outshone his appearance, and as they prepared to mobilise for their long journey to the Belgian frontier the Commanding Officer sought him out. His permanent driver was incapacitated and he needed a replacement. While Ray may not have relished the prospect of being chauffeur, and by virtue of that batman to the CO, he quickly realised it would probably keep him away from the front line. So it was with a certain degree of security that he slid in behind the wheel of the Humber Supersnipe, a radio operator on the seat beside him, and the 'Old Man' ensconced in the rear.

It was highly likely that Ray would have befriended that other private in their small entourage. In his entire professional career he had not once cleaned his own boots, nor the shoes that he would wear outside the stadium. His laundry had always been undertaken by others. Even his overnight bag for the away matches was presented to him packed and ready to go. He was not about to perform such menial tasks for anyone, no matter what his rank. But a few shillings directed to the right palm could solicit the dedicated services of a surrogate batman. Ray may even have been forgiven for thinking that this leisurely motor trip through the French countryside was little more than a Sunday jaunt. A rare letter home to Fanny, although heavily censored, hinted at this disconcern as he recounted a visit to his Aunt Lil, an 'aunt' the family never knew existed. His fumbled attempt at imparting his whereabouts, a contravention of orders that could have resulted in a court-martial, was wasted.

Despite those much earlier reports of bombing forays on the Paris perimeter at the outbreak of war Ray's unit itself had yet to see anything of the enemy. Indeed, the first contingent of 158,000 men in the British Expeditionary Force that had arrived in October 1939 had still to be called into action. Even as the 53rd arrived at their new billet in Lambersart, a short distance from Lille, and took over the 6th Field Regiment's gun positions on the Gort line, defending the Belgian frontier, they had not once fired in anger.

All that was about to change as the 'balloon went up' on 10 May. It was still some time before dawn when the German Foreign Minister, von Ribbentrop, summoned the Belgian and Dutch envoys to his office on Berlin's Wilhelmstrasse. With a deadly straight face and unemotional tone he informed them that German forces were at that very moment crossing the borders of their countries to 'protect their neutrality in the face of an imminent British and French attack'.

The 28 German divisions that had been amassed along a 150-mile front suddenly sprang out of the darkness to bring blitzkrieg to the unprepared Low Countries. Vital bridges and airfields were seized before the defenders were able to go into action. The Dutch contingency plan to open the dykes in the hope that the flooding would keep the Germans at bay was also foiled by the speed of the attack, and the invaders' well-conceived methods of dealing with such inevitability. For fear of offending their pugnacious neighbour the Benelux governments had failed to respond to the Allied intelligence reports or participate in co-ordinated defence measures.

At 5.30 a.m., as those ashen-faced envoys were confronting their antagonist across a polished desk in the heart of the Reich, the British Commander-in-Chief, Lord Gort, received the alert. One hour and fifteen minutes later his forces were ordered into action.

The pre-drawn Allied plan, calling for an Anglo-French force to advance into Belgium and take up positions in support of the Belgian army, would require two days to be put into action for any hope of lasting success. Such time was a luxury to be denied them. Having made the mistake of only lightly defending the natural geographic barrier of the southern Ardennes, the Allies had unwittingly opened an unchallenged corridor for the aggressors. Within hours of the launch the massive Eban Emael fortress at Liège, in the foothills of this vast range, had fallen. By dusk on that first day the Belgian army was already beginning to disintegrate. The Dutch were faring no better. Despite their success in repulsing a German attempt to capture the Hague and seize the royal family, their great port of Rotterdam was on the verge of totally collapsing after being pulverised by a persistent aerial bombardment, which claimed the lives of at least 800 civilians. Against this background of growing military catastrophe, the heartbroken and discredited British Prime Minister, Neville Chamberlain, relinquished his office to the newly elected Winston Churchill.

With the despatches ordering the 53rd into action there arrived a late communication for Jack Hurst. His only son, who was still crying the day they parted company, had died of a burst appendix. In easier times Jack would have been granted compassionate leave. Instead he resolutely mounted his gun in readiness for the defence of freedom.

Four days into the fighting, with Queen Wilhelmina and her family safely evacuated to exile in England, the Dutch forces were ordered to stop fighting. In Belgium the 53rd were detailed to vacate Lambersart and deploy their guns along the River Escaut west of Tournai. As they moved out an officer lingered, in order to secrete the symbolic Regimental drum beneath bales of rotting hay in a disused barn on the outskirts of the village, in the hope that he would be able to return shortly to retrieve it. Having assumed, as in the last war, that the Maginot Line would be the final front between France and Germany, they were ill prepared for the onslaught moving swiftly towards their northern provinces through Luxembourg and Belgium, forcing the Allies to withdraw their remaining armies from the River Dyle to the new front on the Escaut.

In a final gesture as Commander-in-Chief of the Allied Forces, before being replaced by General Weygand, General Maurice Gamelin tried to organise a realignment of his diminishing troops in order to launch a series of counter-attacks against the rapidly advancing German Panzer divisions. For a moment the feint appeared to have worked. The lack of accurate information as to the weaknesses of the Allies caused the German divisional commander, Rommel, to reassess his battle plan in the belief that he had been confronted by as many as five tank divisions, a respite that was to see the embattled Anglo-French forces squeezed into an ever tighter and seemingly inescapable corner.

The 53rd Field Regiment of the Bolton Artillery was now in support of the 126th Infantry Brigade, comprising 1st East Lancs, 5th Border and 5th King's Own regiments, when they arrived at the small but deserted farming community of Froidmont in the early hours of 16 May, fewer than 24 hours after the Germans had officially occupied the Hague. The intensive gunnery training that Harry Goslin and his team had undergone was about to be put to the test. While the gun crews methodically dug the gun emplacement pits and camouflaged them the officer in charge, Captain Wood, went with his opposite number in the 5th Border Regiment to reconnoitre forward infantry positions across the River Escaut, where they were to place the artillery observation post which he was to man all night. The following morning the 'Wanderers' guns were brought into action, loosing their first rounds in anger since the declaration of war, against a virtually unseen enemy. As the 5th Border Regiment moved to form a defensive flank on the far side of the river to the north of nearby Tournai, the 53rd's senior officer once again went forward in order to relocate the observation post so that they could better provide the infantry with that all-important artillery cover. Other batteries within the command of the 53rd now came to their support, while a small contingent moved back into Tournai to reconnoitre suitable vantage points from which to sustain their role in the event of withdrawal. Three such sites were chosen, wired and occupied continuously through to another daybreak.

It was macabrely quiet all day on Saturday 18 May. The officers were able to assess the previous day's action, and even return to their original gun positions on the banks of the River Escaut, unaware that the Germans had already reached St Quentin, barely a hundred kilometres to their rear. This was the lull before the storm.

Shortly after Goslin's registration shoot at 0830 hours on the Sunday morning some 400 enemy infantry were seen advancing over the lower slopes of the Mont St Aubert, an escarpment on the far side of the river that formed the boundary of the city of Tournai. Initially they were to prove to be out of range, but when two high-angle guns opened fire in their direction the 53rd responded, scoring some casualties among the visible German detachment. As the opposing force grew in numbers and strength the Bolton gunners targeted the now visible motor transport, horse-drawn artillery and what appeared to be two new headquarters being established on the very outskirts of the city. A strong head wind was beginning to hamper the guns, causing severe loss of range. Towards the evening this abated and the previously registered targets were effectively engaged. Now only a few hundred yards beyond the far river bank the enemy were falling victim to the artillery's increasingly accurate fire. Only the cover of nightfall prevented further heavy casualties, even though the barrage was sporadically maintained. But the retribution was to be swift and devastating.

A dawn air-raid swooped without warning, leaving no time for the anti-aircraft battery to retaliate. Subsequent dangerously close attacks on their observation posts necessitated a rapid redeployment. While the bulk of the guns were being evacuated, two remained in action to provide distraction and cover rather than effective targeting. Now, under increasing pressure, their ammunition expenditure was to reach dangerously high levels.

In danger of being caught in a pincer movement the 53rd began to withdraw, eventually finding themselves defending an unsatisfactory position in Cysoing, a small town midway between Tournai and the French city of Lille. While further batteries were being located behind a now desolate weaving shed the Liaison Officer went forward to the headquarters of the King's Own Regiment who were themselves being pinned down by heavy fire. The targets they requested the artillery to decommission were beyond their observed fire range, and with concern for the effectiveness of the remaining supply lines they had to decline.

As the virtually unchallenged German advance proceeded across the River Aisne and forward to Amiens on the Somme, just 100 kilometres from Paris, the Bolton Artillery were now coming under increasingly heavy artillery fire from the more effective long-range enemy weapons. With their target still invisible the Commanding Officer took the unprecedented risk of relocating his observation post to a windmill situated on a knoll barely 100 yards behind the front-line trench. While this move enabled the 53rd to sight on the targets requested earlier by the infantry, it also made them a sitting target in return.

The rousing cheers from the terraces and stands of Burnden Park were now fading memories replaced by a near constant roar of gunfire, exploding shells and raging fires, interspersed with tormented cries of human anguish. The air was filled with the stench of cordite. In every direction there was evidence of desperate battles being played out in a scorched summer landscape. They were trapped in a Dante's Inferno, partly of their own making, that melded day into night into day.

An SOS call answered during the night of the 24th had seen them ranging in on a target outside their original zone, and on an unprotected flank, providing further evidence of the enemy surrounding them. The Bolton guns were rapidly manipulated to engage the attackers, necessitating the rear battery firing over the heads of the forward gunners, aiming for this new threat from the dense shrubbery barely 25 yards ahead of them. In the pandemonium during a defensive right sweep one round had hit a tree between the guns, and exploded. As dawn broke the German light artillery now had the range of the windmill and opened fire, an onslaught supported by high-velocity gunfire from the nearby wood. Number 4 gun of the

53rd returned fire with a sustained bombardment of the copse, enabling the observation officer and his support to evacuate the now blazing windmill.

Even as this action continued to rage throughout another day Captain Wood had taken the cross-country route to the next village, Faches-Thumesnil, to reconnoitre for a safe retreat. The batteries were already pulling out, in the direction of Lille, when he returned to encounter a heavy rifle assault that was to pursue their retreat into Lambersart. There was barely time to catch their breath, let alone retrieve the Regimental drum, as they were ordered to move out during the small hours towards Ploegsteert. Once again coming under fire from enemy infantry close to the main road, they broke off their withdrawal to prepare and occupy an observation post to direct their guns at this new threat. The communication link had still to be hooked up when orders were received to move with guns, ammunition and minimum transport towards Dunkirk. All else was to be jettisoned and destroyed. The Commanding Officer pulled his guns out of action, picked up an abandoned Quad (a four by four troop carrier), together with a 25-pounder, and drove on to Rousebrugge-Harinche, as the Luftwaffe added to the nightmare by launching the first of a series of dive-bombing raids that would accompany them all the way to the coast and halfway across the English Channel.

Ernie Forrest's battery was the last to leave. They were still inside the old barn where they had hidden the guns when they became aware that the German's had registered them. Jack Roberts and the remaining gun crew frantically tried to hook up the gun trailer as Ernie leapt into the driving seat and kicked the Quad into life. Jack caught the crunch as Ernie slammed the vehicle into gear, and yelled a warning: 'The doors, Ernie! They're shut!'

'Sod the doors,' screamed Ernie, 'the Germans are coming.' Jack just managed to hurl himself onto the rapidly accelerating vehicle when Ernie smashed it through the timber doors and sped off into the night.

'Suddenly, without prior consultation, with the least possible notice, without the advice of his Ministers, upon his own personal act, King Leopold of Belgium sent a plenipotentiary to the German command surrendering his Army and exposing the whole Allied flank without the means of retreat . . . All would have shared the fate to which King Leopold had condemned the finest army his country had ever formed.' These harsh words were delivered to the House of Commons by Winston Churchill exactly one week after the Bolton Artillery and the entire British Expeditionary Force began their flight to freedom.

With communication now severed between the three main Allied armies it could easily have become an uncontrollable rout. A vast German force was mobilised along their eastern flank, separating them from the now capitulated Belgians. Survivors of the French military were filtering in from the west, under pressure from the Nazi might prodding their rear. A steel barrier of mechanised weaponry was thrown up along the entire thirty-mile length of the only corridor still open for the exodus. On the coast the Germans now occupied the port of Boulogne, forcing these retreating armies into a confined killing field that was the open plains and sand dunes of Dunkirk.

There was chaos, but no panic. Arriving in Rousebrugge-Harinche 'A' troop of the 53rd took up open anti-tank positions to cover troops defending the River Yser. Without the time or equipment to establish an effective observation post the Bolton Artillery began shelling the advancing German infantry and tanks over open sights. No sooner had they gone into action than they received a despatch ordering them to the coast. Three guns had already disengaged and moved out when the orders were rescinded. With seriously reduced resources Goslin and his companions attempted to remain engaged well into the night, even through a temporary malfunction of one of the guns and with visibility down to fewer than one hundred yards. In a momentary lull in the fighting they realised that the other batteries, with whom they had lost radio communication, had pulled out. The remaining gunners disengaged and recommenced their procession to the coast, hoping they would regain contact with the rest of the Regiment.

It seemed that every artery to that narrow strip of shoreline was now clogged. Soldiers separated from their units were swept along with the tide of refugees. A carnival of assorted vehicles transported their lives to uncertainty. The flotilla of small craft that was scheduled to arrive in the shallow waters off Brayes Dunes on 30 May was commissioned to evacuate armed personnel only. There would be no such escape for civilians.

Breaking out of their near encirclement in the middle of the night Ernie Forrest was confused. He was in alien territory on a starless night. All road signs had been removed to confound the enemy. Like the majority of his fellow servicemen Ernie had never before heard of Dunkirk, nor in which direction it lay. Stan Hanson was in a similar quandary when he finally made it on to a metal road in the driving seat of an ammunition truck, Donny Howe beside him and a whole platoon in the back. Acting on impulse he swung the truck on to the disconcertingly quiet highway, littered with the burnt-out debris of a defeated army, and gunned the vehicle into top gear. Rounding a corner at speed he all but slammed head-on into a German tank, an entire division roaring in convoy behind it. The soldiers were flung violently against the metal ribcage supporting the vulnerable canvas cover as Stan deftly spun the groaning machine into a 360-degree turn. Skidding on the verge he lost control as a shell spent itself harmlessly across their stern. Before another round could be fired Stan ditched the truck in the culvert. His cargo of battered and frightened men dived into the field, grabbing what hand-held weapons they could, and fled for the cover of nearby woods. Stan and Donny paused just long enough to loose several rounds of light-bore ammunition into the engine block, to permanently disable the vehicle. Ducking and weaving they disappeared into the night aware of machine-gun fire opening up behind them. Stan and Donny had been mates for years, sharing everything. On match days they would share digs. They had even been known to share a bed when there was a house full. Now they were sharing the most frightening experience of their lives.

Ray Westwood was driving like a man possessed. There was little other traffic on the road. This should have alerted him to the dangers ahead. The radio operator had lost contact with the main body of the Regiment as soon as they had vacated their last position under heavy enemy fire. Even the officer's maps were useless. The columns of erect poplars flashing by on either side gave the illusion of barrelling through a cavernous gorge, devoid of landmarks. They were aware of the sounds of battle, but were unable to determine from which direction they were erupting. Without warning a blacked-out motorcycle speeding from the opposite direction slewed across the road barely fifty yards in front of them. In Ray's heightened state of concentration he was able to react instantaneously, avoiding a head-on collision. The despatch rider extricated himself from his machine and ran to the staff car.

'The Krauts are only one mile up this road,' he warned. 'You wanna get the f— out of here.'

The last words had already faded into the night as Ray slammed the vehicle into gear, pushed his foot to the floor and threw the heavy car around. He was already accelerating back into the unknown darkness before the despatch rider was able to remount his own machine and head in desperate pursuit.

As the sun rose on what was to be a glorious summer's day the first wave of Stukas descended on the defenceless straggle of soldiers and civilians pushing towards Dunkirk. The nerve-shattering shriek as the planes commenced their dive had their helpless victims abandon their vehicles and hurl themselves into the roadside ditches. For what seemed like eternity the bombs rained down, vehicles exploded, people screamed and the sun was blotted out behind a billowing cloud of black smoke. Just as it cleared and the survivors began to drift back on to the scene to assess the damage the planes returned to strafe them with machine-gun fire.

Responding to a nearby raid Goslin arrested his battery beside a dressing station, and prepared to provide defensive cover while the medical staff performed critical last-minute tasks before relocating. This may have been a textbook exercise, but experience told the doctor in charge that the presence of artillery would cancel the protection afforded by the huge red cross emblazoned across his tent. Even as he was imploring the battery to move on a reconnaissance plane swooped low overhead discharging its ominous plume of white exhaust smoke that would direct the following bombers to their new target.

'Ranji' Hawarden had become isolated from his men shortly after this attack. Ahead of him at a village crossroads a heavily armed German patrol was roughly interrogating the stream of civilians, flinging open coats, desperately searching for straggling soldiers concealed within their midst. The French peasants huddled around him. Convinced he would be captured Ranji inched into a passage between two cottages. Carelessly discarded against the rear wall was a battered motorcycle. To his amazement it kicked into life. Ignoring the guttural screams and ensuing gunfire he sped across the fields and on to a rutted farm track. Unaware whether he was being pursued or not he sped between the waving fronds of wheat, and through a thick copse before finally emerging in a small clearing dominated by a well secluded farmhouse. A curtain shuddered. Having made a poor attempt at concealing the motorcycle he approached the building. Before he could knock at the door it crept open and Ranji was confronted by a gnarled farmer, a shotgun firmly aimed at Ranji's head. Behind the weather-beaten old man a chorus of inquisitive girls leered at Ranji. Having scanned the horizon to see if the British officer had been followed by the Nazis the farmer beckoned him inside. Ranji almost broke into laughter at the formal confrontation with this man's 11 comely daughters, bringing so many barrack room jokes flooding back involuntarily into his memory.

The atmosphere was tense. But whether the farmer was more concerned for his daughters' collective chastity or the imminent arrival of a German patrol in pursuit of the officer, Ranji would never have the opportunity to ascertain. From his very limited knowledge of French he soon realised that they were suggesting he should hide in the 'priest hole' cavity carved into the foundation soil and accessed via a hatch beneath the wood burning stove, until the threat had passed. The tension mounted as the sounds of approaching vehicles disturbed the air. Unable to fit into the confined space, 'Ranji' was not about to jeopardise this family for his own safety. With garbled thanks he slipped out the back door and sprinted towards the woods, straight into the arms of a foraging unit of German infantry, and five years of captivity as an inmate of Stalag 383.

The Regiment was completely and irretrievably dispersed by the time Captain Wood arrived with his Quad at Les Moeres on the outer edge of the Dunkirk perimeter. The area was criss-crossed with a network of canals that were to prove vital to the British eleventh-hour defence. Leaving two guns and what remained of his element of the 53rd he went to recce. More and more troops were pouring into the area as the German infantry and Panzer divisions closed in on all sides. On finding Brigadier Marshall the Captain was given orders to bring his guns into action against the swarm of heavy armour that was opposing them across the Bergues Furnes Canal. Having sent a despatch rider back for the guns Captain Wood was devastated to learn that the two remaining batteries under his command had received counter orders to destroy their weapons and proceed to the beach head. Of no further assistance to the Brigadier, who only moments before had received his own orders to embark with the HQ 42nd Division, Wood penetrated deeper inside the perimeter in search of the Bolton Artillery. Crossing over the Canal Des Chats, which was destined to become their final front line, he successfully met up with a detachment of 'C' troop. Their remaining four guns included 210 Battery, manned by four Bolton Wanderers under their own captain, Harry Goslin. Now attached to the remnants of the 27th Field Regiment they had got themselves into an anti-tank position on the road between Tleegervelt and Teteghem.

Ray Westwood and the CO had arrived in the area in the early hours of the same morning and had immediately gone in search of the Bolton Artillery, a hopeless task in the midst of such confusion and constant attack. It was already evening before they located what they believed to be a field HQ. An armed sentry was posted beside the entrance to the bombed-out farmhouse. Alighting from his vehicle the CO requested to see the intelligence officer.

'It's not that sort of headquarters, Sir. But there is a guards officer inside,' responded the private, as if still on duty at their home barracks.

The CO, feeling that this officer would be able to provide little help in locating his own troops, prepared to return to the car, but was pressed by the sentry to at least make himself known to the guards officer, who would be offended if he did not. On entering the premises it must have seemed like a scene from a comic. The house had been severely damaged by both artillery and small arms fire, but an area of the main room had been cleared of all signs of battle. All that remained was a solid wood dining-table, now laid with a veritable banquet. The wine had been consumed, but the officer was graciously able to offer the CO a glass of excellent port.

Shortly after this disorientating encounter they finally made contact with the remains of their unit. Ray was immediately relieved of his duties to the CO, ostensibly to enable him to perform the function of a despatch rider. It was while engaged in this activity between the 27th and the 53rd that he was happily reunited with Harry Goslin, a reunion that was to be marked by the commencement of their most concentrated defensive bombardment of the conflict. For more than 24 hours they were to sustain their assault of the relentlessly advancing Panzer divisions and supporting infantry. With limited resources available to them they were only able to establish an observation post less than half a mile in front of the guns, resulting in very close-quarter artillery fire. The whole area where they were dug in was subjected to continuous shelling, from all calibres up to six-inch. German infantry guns joining the attack from a position within the nearby Warhem church tower soon fell victim to the effective shooting of Harry Goslin's 210 Battery, who scored 12 direct hits.

It was Saturday 1 June, and the front page of the *Bolton Evening News* carried the story of the 'Fight For Goals' at the League War Cup semi-final between Blackburn and Newcastle at Ewood Park, alongside the first clear reports of the action across the Channel. Lord Gort was already home and being honoured by the King, who conferred on him the GCB (Grand Cross of the Bath, a meritorious knighthood). 'That gallant force of British and French comrades who have stood shoulder to shoulder against fearful odds defending the "Corunna Line" in order to save the British Expeditionary Force from annihilation are now making their final stand ready for the moment when they themselves will crown this supreme feat of arms by a dash to the coast.' For the young Nat Lofthouse, who had trained

There was chaos but no panic when the BEF began their retreat to Dunkirk. Here an immaculately attired sergeant leads an orderly march to the coast.

Many vehicles were immobilised and abandoned at the roadside as the arteries became choked.

These antiquated French gun trailers served to add to the congestion of the roads to Dunkirk.

French horse-drawn vehicles also served to snarl up the narrow streets of the French villages through which the retreating armies had to pass.

Retreat to Dunkirk.

Donny Howe and Stan Hanson had yet
to see action in this new theatre of war
when they posed for this photo in Cairo,
on 26 September 1942.

Stan and Donny rounded up some other soldiers from the 53rd for this stage-managed group shot in Cairo. (*left to right*) back row: Jack Roberts, Val Thompson, Stan Hanson, unknown. Front row: George Catterall, Donny Howe, Ernie Forrest.

Jack Hurst outside the National Sporting Club, Gezira Island, Cairo, the venue for another Wanderers victory.

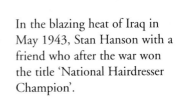

In the blazing heat of Iraq in May 1943, Stan Hanson with a friend who after the war won the title 'National Hairdresser Champion'.

Stan and the unknown soldier in Naples, 1945. Tragically the man died the day after this photograph was taken.

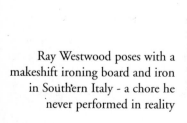

Ray Westwood poses with a makeshift ironing board and iron in Southern Italy - a chore he never performed in reality

Jack Hurst and George Catterall in Florence, 1945, sometime after the Germans had finally surrendered.

Stan Hanson managed to rustle up a passable uniform to participate in a guard of honour for a Gurkha who was to be awarded the Victoria Cross for extreme valour.

Despite hating every minute of army life Ray Westwood could not resist a beaming smile as he posed with soldiers from the 53rd on the banks of the Suez on the day they arrived in Egypt.

A shell-ridden gun position which was occupied in snow and mud for three months during the winter of 1944. The snow-capped Apennines can just be seen in the background.

Bolton Wanderers beat Manchester United to win this last wartime trophy, The Football League (War) Cup North.

Harry Hubbick managed to play continuously throughout the war whilst maintaining his reserved occupation as a miner. He was rewarded with the team captaincy.

Record crowds gather on the embankment terraces for the cup tie against Stoke City on 6 March 1946, in the revived FA Cup tournament. The expressions reveal a mix of excitement and apprehension.

As the crush becomes greater the police and the St John's Ambulancemen move to the edge of the terraces to help people out. Several spectators have clambered onto a locomotive shunted onto the siding outside the ground.

Disaster! A startled referee accompanies a police officer to the scene of the tragedy.

ABOVE: The 1946/47 Bolton Wanderers team captained by Jack Atkinson . . . although the after effects of the war were taking their toll . . . only six pre-war players made the grade.

RIGHT: Jack Atkinson started the war in the police force but later joined the army and was to fight alongside the 'Wartime Wanderers' in Italy.

LEFT

TOP: Despite the disaster at Burnden Park on 6 March, Bolton Wanderers went through to the FA Cup semi-final against Charlton, where Stan Hanson tangled with their striker.

BOTTOM: The start of the first full season after the war saw the repeat of the fixture list abandoned in 1939. Ray Westwood and Nat Lofthouse look on anxiously as the Portsmouth goalkeeper prevents an early goal in the third match of the season.

The Regimental Drum resplendent in new livery at the Bolton Artillery museum

Roll of Honour on the wall of the
TA Bolton Artillery Drill Hall.

Lieutenant Harry Goslin was
buried in Vasto, Italy, close to
where he was killed in action,
December 1943.

Stan Hanson, still training and
playing five years after the war . . .

. . . had lost none of his form, as he
clearly displayed in a home match
against Blackpool, October 1949.

rigorously throughout the season despite not having played a proper match, the editorial in the *Olympians Corner* was probably of more importance to him.

There was growing doubt in the minds of many big football clubs as to the chance they would have of staging an attractive competition for the next season. The Football League had suggested a scheme embracing four divisions, geographically split, but this had not met with approval. Similarly, Manchester City's proposal for clubs to be divided into five sections had yet to gain any significant support. But the main cause for concern was the ability of professional clubs to raise an effective team now that the calling-up of men for active service was in full swing. Admittedly some clubs had benefited from their players being employed in reserved occupations, but for others, like Bolton Wanderers, whose players were already embroiled in the fighting, the struggle to keep going was rapidly worsening. In making every effort to fulfil their obligations the clubs would become increasingly dependent on players such as Nat and his contemporaries. But what might have been misconstrued as a criticism was actually an accolade, for it would fall to these juveniles to keep the national sport alive for the duration of the hostilities. A fact that was not missed by The Olympian in his conclusion: 'Their teams may be weakened by the introduction of so many young and inexperienced players, but they will have the good wishes of every patriot.'

Meanwhile ships of every kind were continuously arriving at the south-east coastal ports, their decks crammed with more officers and men of the BEF and French Army, each with their own harrowing tale to tell. A boatload of dusky French colonials spoke of their desperate fighting right up to the point of embarkation. There were disturbing stories of ships being sunk by heavy bombing, and of the survivors being machine-gunned as they desperately thrashed about in the polluted waters in search of some life raft or floating debris to save them.

A war correspondent appeared through the smoke of battle and captured Harry Goslin and his battery for posterity. The photograph would be rolling off the *Daily Express* presses even before Goslin was back in Blighty. The celebrity missing from this archival portrait was Ray Westwood, who was taking an urgent despatch to the 27th Field Regiment's CO with a request for more ammunition, which was hastily met.

'The epic withdrawal goes on,' reported the *BEN*, 'and there are still high hopes that it will be consummated by saving the greater part of those who were prepared to sacrifice their lives in order that their comrades may be saved.' At the time of this publication some unofficial estimates claimed that there was no more than one Allied division still remaining in Flanders.

Smoke belching from the fires now blazing a trail along the entire front line was making observation for potential artillery targets virtually impossible. At the request of the last wave of infantry to pass through Goslin opened fire on two very vague objectives. All that remained was for the batteries to sustain harassing fire directed solely by map references, in order to allow these last few men to escape.

There was a crush on the small pontoon bridge over the final canal before Brayes Dunes. Word was filtering back through the lines that the last boats were leaving. In his concerted effort to reach the shore with the handful of comrades still with him, Sergeant Killan stumbled and fell into the canal, now littered with ditched hardware and corpses. His fall was broken across the barrel of a discarded 25-pounder and he could sense his lower spine shattering. He was paralysed with pain, and resigned himself to his fate. Against his express wishes a couple of soldiers from the 53rd leapt from the bridge to his rescue. In a state of near delirium he was hauled on to the banks, and virtually frog-marched to that last vessel.

Major Wingfield, commanding 'C' troop of the 53rd, was now under the impression that no more ships would be coming and so braced himself for the possibility of surrender. It may have been Westwood's sudden return with news that embarkation had ceased at Brayes Dunes but was still continuing from Dunkirk that prompted him to go to the beaches.

Arriving at the beach head in the late afternoon it was apparent from the activity and the orderly queues filing into the sea that evacuation was still under way, despite the continuous bombing and strafing by the Luftwaffe that was now being joined by the German heavy artillery ranged along the coastline from Boulogne. Many held their ground, refusing to relinquish their positions in the line. Men fell, dead or injured, but the pace continued. Others leapt from the lone jetty in desperation, their limbs twisting and bodies contorting as they plunged into the heaving waters. Westwood dove headlong into a slit trench dug into the dunes. As sand and shrapnel erupted dangerously close to his shelter others piled in after him. He was later to say, 'I'd never mind how many were on top of me, so long as I were on bottom when the bombs fell.'

Wingfield grabbed the nearest officer and asked where he would

have to report and was directed to a ramshackle hut that was acting
as the HQ. Once inside he requested the order of embarkation, and
was shocked to discover that the Bolton Artillery was nowhere to be
found on their lists. Having ensured them they were very much in
existence, the Major was told they could embark after the Coldstream
Guards. As luck would have it the first officer Wingfield met on
emerging from the hut was the gentleman from this very regiment with
whom he had taken a glass of port. Quickly he imparted the orders,
requesting that the Bolton Artillery be informed via their despatch
rider, whose head was still firmly buried in the sand, when the Guards'
embarkation was imminent in order that the 53rd may follow. The
officer puffed himself up with pride and demanded the reverse order
of departure with the pompous declaration, 'Nobody follows the
Coldstream Guards.' Not wishing to enter into an argument, whatever
the priorities of rank, Major Wingfield returned to the front line. The
last remaining guns and vehicles of the 53rd Field Regiment, Bolton
Artillery were destroyed, and at 2100 hours on 1 June the exhausted
gun crews marched on Dunkirk. During that final 24 hours of battle
they had put in an exemplary performance, successfully halting the
German advance.

    Stan Hanson and Donny Howe had made it on foot to the beaches
and were now entrenched with the remnants of an infantry unit.
Unbeknown to them Ernie Forrest was also bedded down in the sand
that night. In the flight they had lost virtually all of their belongings
and equipment. As darkness fell the air assault on the beaches eased
up, but the sounds of battle could still be heard, even the occasional
sniper shot. Stan lay motionless; a strange searchlight shone at his feet,
making him a positive target if he were to stray into its beam. When
day broke Stan was shocked to discover the soldier next to him was
dead, from a single bullet. There was little time to contemplate his own
luck as there began a mad scramble; a Major ran along the beach
rousing the remaining troops and ordering them to the sea, with the
ominous instruction that no one would be allowed to embark without
a weapon. Fortunately this was the one possession both Stan and
Donny had held close to themselves throughout their entire ordeal. But
Ernie had to scour the carnage and debris of numerous air attacks until
he was able to retrieve a weapon the previous owner would no longer
miss.

    As they plunged into the sea the first of the day's air-raids began.
Ernie's athletic legs pumped through the water as spray from a nearby
explosion washed over him. The waves from the aftershock saw him

tumble into the surf. His objective, a small coastal steamer, was about to pull away to escape this bombardment. Ernie discarded his weapon and powered through the water. As the propeller began to create a wake at the stern a khaki-clad arm reached down from the lower deck. Ernie clasped the man's wrist and could feel himself rising from the waters as the boat ploughed into the crests. There was a pause in Ernie's upward momentum. The officer at the other end of the arm nodded in the direction of the shallows.

'I believe you've forgotten something.'

Ernie's glare burnt into him. 'If you want the sodding gun, you sodding well go and get it.'

Stan and Donny had also managed to survive the bombing and found themselves rowing for all their might towards the only destroyer in the rapidly diminishing fleet. Everyone knew that it was now or never. Unless they escaped on one of the ships still bobbing offshore they would be ensnared by the enemy. More and more soldiers pulled themselves into the frail craft. Stan and Donny kept their heads down, well aware that as long as they were in charge of the oars they were indispensable. They even managed to stay detached when a young commissioned officer rose in the prow of the boat, brandishing his pistol and threatening to shoot anyone else who attempted to board the frail craft which was clearly in danger of sinking. Without a word being spoken a huddle of privates leapt in unison and bundled the startled officer into the sea. He was still floundering and screaming threats as they pulled away.

Miraculously, Stan and Donny made it on to the *Winchelsea*, exhausted but uninjured, and still with the rifles they had been carrying religiously since Lambersart. Wrapped in blankets and being led to the galley for hot drinks, and the first food for what seemed an eternity, they finally relinquished their weapons. Some time later, invigorated by the welcome sustenance provided compliments of the Royal Navy, they returned to reclaim the armour that was to be their landing pass in England, only to find the guns had been stolen.

It was to be another long and tense day for Harry Goslin and the very last unit of Bolton artillerymen. Having found a cache of food they had dug in near the base of the mole that meandered into the sea and awaited news of that night's evacuation programme. In those last 24 hours on the guns Harry was to be credited with four enemy tanks destroyed, a fact that was to contribute significantly to his battlefield commission.

The Germans intensified their savage onslaught on Dunkirk,

although their main thrust was now towards Paris, their objective the complete capitulation of the country.

Shortly before midnight on Sunday 2 June Harry Goslin and his men embarked on the gunboat HMS *Locust*.

In what was to be one of the last French war communiqués before the German occupation their government paid high tribute to the supreme efforts of these Allied soldiers: 'This retreat, accomplished by troops pressed upon from all sides, deprived of all rest for 20 days, and suddenly left uncovered on their left by the surrender of King Leopold, will remain a heroic example of tenacity in the history of the French and British armies.'

That night Operation Dynamo was terminated.

FIVE

Like thousands of others all over Great Britain, the loved ones of the 53rd Field Regiment RA anxiously awaited news of their menfolk's safe return home from the bloodied beaches of northern France. The football supporters of Bolton also kept a keen eye out for stories of their heroes' progress on the battlefield. Slowly the word began to filter out that the Wartime Wanderers had not only done their Regiment, town and country proud but had often exceeded the call of duty and earned the respect and admiration of their military colleagues.

Immediately after the flotilla of small boats had delivered them to safety the Bolton players were transported to a holding camp on the Salisbury Plain for a short enforced rest period before being moved to Newcastle upon Tyne on 1 July 1940. The *Bolton Evening News* published an announcement from a Bolton Wanderers board meeting at which the club chairman, Mayor Entwhistle, had been able to report that all the first-team players had returned safely to England.

A copy of this notification was sent to Sam Westwood in Brierley Hill, and while he was pleased to learn that no harm had befallen his son he was disappointed to have heard it from a third party. Ray Westwood was always more a man of action than letters and his level of correspondence from the trenches would never amount to much. But in this instance the army had provided Ray, as they had every soldier, with a pre-paid postcard that only required his signature. Even this was never sent. Now that his family knew Ray was safe his wife and his mother began to ponder what possible effects the army life, and in particular this latest horrific adventure, may have had on their free-spirited boy. Ray's lack of domestic skills was legendary. His father cleaned his shoes, his mother waited on him hand and foot, and his wife had found herself slotting neatly into this established routine well before she tripped down the aisle with him. Fanny had accepted that most of these chores fell within a woman's domain, but she did once ask why Ray would never clean his own footwear, only to be told that it was far easier to have his shoes polished for him than for Fanny to spend half the night scrubbing shoe polish off the cuffs of his shirt. So the thought of Ray sitting in some alien barracks cleaning and polishing the army kit of his Commanding Officer afforded the women much amusement. They were even cheered by the prospect that the army would quite possibly deliver them back a son and a husband finally capable of tending to his own domestic needs.

Even if his written communication was to all intents and purposes non-existent Ray Westwood did hold his home and family close to his heart. While in transit from Salisbury Plain to Newcastle by train Ray realised that the journey would take him virtually past his own front door, and his new bride. A passioned appeal was made to the officer in charge who agreed to turn a blind eye to Ray making a short detour to Brierley Hill during the three-hour halt scheduled at neighbouring Birmingham. Ray's parents and wife were absolutely overjoyed when he knocked on the door and surprised them with a quick impromptu visit. Their joy was not even dented when the heavy kit bag that he deposited on the kitchen table turned out to be full of dirty washing to be done before he rejoined the train. It was a happy moment. Same old Ray, safe and sound in Brierley Hill, with a pile of laundry he needed doing in order to smarten himself up before his next parade. Not a word was said of his baptism under fire.

Similar reunions were to be enjoyed by the families, wives and girlfriends of all the Wartime Wanderers during those first few weeks of summer. Ernie Forrest's mum went to visit her youngest of nine children as soon as she had received his card. He had not been home on leave once since his call-out, and she was concerned. She need not have been. Ernie had used his humour to great effect as a foil against the harsh realities of an army at war, realities that came home with a thumping blow when he learnt from his mother that his eldest brother, Anthony, had been killed when his ship was sunk bringing soldiers back from Dunkirk. Harry Goslin returned home to his wife and two sons in Bolton with a new honour to his name. Harry's exploits on the gun battery at Dunkirk and his displays of leadership and courage on the battlefield had earned him a full military promotion to the commissioned rank of Lieutenant.

The usual army procedure following such a promotion from the ranks to officer status was for the new appointee to be transferred out of the unit. This was in recognition of the fact that it was often difficult for an officer to command a body of men with whom he had lived and fought alongside as an equal. Harry Goslin's superiors realised that his was a special case. Harry had in effect been commanding his team-mates as their captain on the field for many years. All of the Wanderers players and now all of his barrack-room comrades had the utmost respect for Goslin and his style of leadership. Therefore the exceptional decision was taken to allow Lieutenant Harry Goslin to remain with the 53rd Field Regiment and to lead his unit from the front as he had always done with the Bolton Wanderers.

While the players had been away at training camp and in France life for those who had remained at home in Bolton had settled into a wartime routine. People went about their lives in as normal a way as possible during daylight hours, but their nightlife was to be partially curtailed by the enforced blackout times that were printed daily in the *Bolton Evening News*. The earlier wartime restrictions imposed on public gatherings and entertainments had been relaxed after the first two months. As a consequence League football had returned to Burnden Park in an organised form, although the friendly fixtures lacked that competitive edge the spectators wanted to see. Often games were slow moving, with players choosing to display their ball skills rather than adopting a win-at-all-costs attitude. Everyone concerned with the game recognised the need to revamp the sport so that matches were once more played with points at stake and League positions to vie for.

Football League meetings had been taking place frequently since their plans for a regional competition had first been announced way back in October 1939. Of the existing 88 members of the League who were eligible to play in the proposed wartime contest only six – Aston Villa, Exeter, Derby County, Gateshead, Ipswich and Sunderland – declined the invitation to compete. The new-look League, which was structured on a regional basis with eight divisions, took no account of a club's pre-war standing. Consequently, Bolton Wanderers found themselves in the twelve-team North West Division as one of four First Division clubs alongside two from the Second Division and six from the Third Division North. However, because of the guesting systems these lesser clubs were now able to field big-name players providing a much more engaging spectator sport than the endless rounds of friendly fixtures.

Charles Foweraker was pleased that his predictions about a return to League football had turned out to be accurate. Worthy competition was desperately needed to bring in the crowds. Although Foweraker himself was still working for nothing the club was obligated to pay the players and maintain Burnden Park. In this respect it was painfully obvious that the friendly games were not attracting enough paying spectators to keep the club on a viable financial footing. As part of its plan the Football League had made a ruling concerning the allocation of gate receipts: five per cent of all takings would be remitted to the League for expenses, while the balance would be divided equally between the two competing clubs.

The outstanding issue of the rights of season ticket holders who had purchased before the war still needed to be resolved, especially as this was a problem hanging over the heads of all professional clubs which could ill afford to offer any kind of financial compensation when the drastically reduced gate revenues were already pushing many of them into debt. The situation came to an open confrontation in Bolton when a season ticket holder sued the football club under the Trade Descriptions Act, claiming that he had been unable to watch any of the published league matches for which he had purchased a book of advance tickets. The matter went before the courts with the whole of the football world watching. The outcome of the case was a compromise. The court wisely ruled that a season ticket could be used for all War League games involving the club that had issued it. This decision saved the Football League members literally thousands of pounds, and enabled many to continue competing in the new leagues.

Once the new League structure had been formally announced Charles Foweraker began working on his plan to rebuild the Bolton Wanderers first team. The nucleus was still those players who had remained employed on the home front: Atkinson, Goodall, Hunt and the new captain, Harry Hubbick. They were now to be joined by Foweraker's first batch of young talent who had yet to attain military age. This group, which numbered among its members Jim Connor and A. Burgess, also still included 'Alphabet' Jones who had signed for the Territorials along with Harry Goslin. So it was a foregone conclusion that his residency would be short-lived. But there were others in the wings, including Nat Lofthouse, who was being groomed for future stardom, and one Walter Sidebottom, a young left-winger who had made his debut appearance in the first team's 3–0 home victory over Birmingham City in the closing stages of the previous season. Sidebottom was an exceptionally talented player for whom the War League provided the outlet for expression that was to impress not only Foweraker but other team selectors.

On the field the 1939/40 season of War League football had been a successful one for Bolton Wanderers. Of the 22 matches played they won 13, drew four and lost only five to finish in overall fourth position. George Hunt repeated his pre-war season's achievement of being top scorer, with the new discovery Walter Sidebottom coming in a close second, including a memorable four-goal tally in their 8–1 defeat of Southport. Despite this record in adverse conditions, and the fact that all bar one of the home games had ended in victory, the public were still not attending the matches in sufficient numbers to make running the club an economically viable proposition. The harsh facts were that the last two matches at Burnden Park, against the League leaders Bury, and Accrington Stanley, had produced gates of only 950 and 500 respectively. Bolton Wanderers' board of directors were seriously concerned about the club's future and had some difficult decisions to make.

Charles Foweraker still held the firm conviction that the club's long-term prospects would only be secured by persevering with playing football at Burnden Park. The fiscal reality was that the club could not even afford the running costs that this required. In addition to the players' wages and the day-to-day administrative costs associated with the organisation of matches the club also had to pay for water, electricity, rates and insurance. In the summer of 1940 in the wake of the Dunkirk retreat and amid the first threatening rumblings of the blitz, Bolton Wanderers had their darkest hour. The board of directors decided not to compete in the War League competition of 1940/41 and the club was closed down. Bolton Wanderers Football Club had finally succumbed to the pressures of war. The gates of Burnden Park were locked and the shutters put up.

At the age of 63 and after 45 years of continuous service at Burnden Park Charles Foweraker was left without a team to manage. Electricity and water supplies to the ground were cut off and the empty terraces were utilised by the Ministry of Supply to store food and provisions. The one silver lining to this dark cloud was that the pitch was maintained in a serviceable condition to be used by the Education Authority. Foweraker was to spend many long days alone at the ground in what must have appeared to many as a futile attempt to keep the club alive. Nat Lofthouse must also have felt that his chance of glory on the pitch at Burnden Park would never come to fruition and that he was destined to remain at Peter Caffery and Sons, the reed manufacturers to the mills, for whom he had been working since leaving school.

It has to be said that the apparent apathy of Bolton's football supporters should be put in context. Events in France had been at the forefront of people's minds. Every day the *Bolton Evening News* had brought word of the worsening situation. The British and French armies had their backs to the wall and for several weeks it looked as if the battle for France would not only be lost but virtually the entire British Expeditionary Force would be annihilated. With the Bolton Artillery in the midst of this carnage the town could only wait anxiously for the slightest glimmer of hope. It came on Tuesday 10 June 1940 when the Prime Minister, Winston Churchill, made a statement to the House of Commons: 'When, a week ago today, I asked the House to fix this afternoon for a statement I feared it would be my hard lot to announce the greatest military disaster in our long history. The whole root and core of the British Army seemed about to perish upon the field or to be led into ignominious and starving captivity.' In fact the amazing armada of over one thousand small ships had saved the lives of three hundred and thirty-five thousand Allied troops and lifted the mood of the nation. If ever there was a turning point in war this was it. June 1940 saw the embodiment of the nation's strength of character manifest itself in the Dunkirk spirit.

Winston Churchill set about steeling the nation for their next great challenge when he warned that the 'Battle of Britain' was about to commence, and preparations should proceed for the defence of the country. Any obstacle that would make life difficult for intruders on British soil was put in place. But as Boltonians were to discover, this also made life very difficult for those already living there. It became a criminal offence to leave a car unlocked or a bicycle unattended. All the road signs, railway station names and shop names bearing the identity of the town were removed. Bus destinations became the name of a local pub or other landmark rather than the name of a town or village. This campaign was so successful that when one German pilot crash-landed in Britain he remembered being confused as to why, on his way to prison camp, every railway station he passed through was called Bovril.

The morning of 10 July 1940 was a typical English summer's day. The sun was struggling against intermittent rain showers and flying conditions were less than ideal. This, however, was the day that the Battle of Britain began, bringing the British civilian population face to face with the enemy. Not only did the Royal Air Force have to contend with the Luftwaffe fighters but the principal cities of the country found themselves targets for the massive bombing campaign known as the Blitz.

Dunkirk had been a traumatic experience for all those involved. It brought home to the volunteers exactly what they had joined up for all those months ago. Bolton's goalkeeper, Stan Hanson, was usually the calmest of men. All who knew him described him as a gentle giant. Calm under pressure, and a calming influence on all those around him. Shortly after arriving in England, following the Dunkirk evacuation, Stan had learned that over the coming weeks they were all to be allowed a four-day leave. May Hanson can remember her husband talking anxiously in his sleep during that leave period. Stan was repeating, over and over during the night, '16, and I'm in the last bloody 16'. May asked him in the morning what he had been dreaming about. Stan told her that after the leave had been announced in the camp the men had been sent away in small groups. Eventually there were just 16 left at the camp. Stan, anxious to get home to his wife, had been held back to the last 16 leave places for the entire camp.

Although leave was a welcome break from army life for Stan Hanson it was no rest from the war. The period immediately after Dunkirk was dominated by the aerial threat from German bombers. Bolton itself was not a primary target and in fact only suffered serious bomb damage on a couple of occasions throughout the duration of the war. For Liverpool, though, the Blitz was a daunting time. Due to the strategic importance of the docks and canals the city was constantly bombed during the latter half of 1940 and early 1941. May Hanson, who had returned to Liverpool to live with her mother when Stan was posted, remembers many nights when the air-raid sirens would sound at six o'clock in the evening and the bombardment would be relentless until 5 a.m. the next morning. On one particular leave Stan Hanson was, as usual, staying with May at her mother's house. It was a week-long leave, but by the Wednesday Stan was so tired of the continual night-time bombing that he suggested to May that they go to Manchester to escape the Blitz, book into a hotel and enjoy a few days' peace and quiet. No sooner had they arrived in Manchester than the bombs started dropping on the docklands there as well. By the end of the week Stan said to May, 'I reckon I'm safer with the army than on leave,' and he returned to his unit for a well earned rest!

The 53rd Field Regiment spent the rest of 1940 and the whole of 1941 at various army camps around Britain well away from the Luftwaffe targets. Their monotonous routine comprised a mix of training and Home Guard duties. As the months passed the Wartime Wanderers were to spend their time building coastal defence constructions, manning anti-aircraft batteries and patrolling potential enemy landing sites all along the East Anglia coastline, variously stationed at Beccles, Nancton and Holt.

Most of the leave passes granted to the Bolton artillerymen were of such short duration they allowed insufficient time to travel by public transport to their home town and back. Therefore it was often left to the wives and families to make the journey for the chance of a day or two together. But even the pursuit of an innocent pastime such as a weekend with a loved one was not without its dangers during 1940. While the regiment was in East Anglia May Hanson had decided to travel down from Liverpool to meet her husband during one of his 48-hour leaves. They had chosen to spend the weekend in the quiet little town of Sherringham in Norfolk. During the afternoon of the day she arrived May was walking along the picturesque high street, looking in the shop windows as she whiled away the time until Stan could meet her, totally oblivious to the noise of an approaching aircraft. Alarmed by the shouts of the people around her she turned to see all the locals diving for the nearest shelter. In the nick of time May backed quickly into a covered doorway from where she witnessed in fear the machine-gun fire from a diving Messerschmitt tearing into the tarmac of the road before her. Shaken by this close call the Hansons reflected that they were destined never to avoid the war wherever they went in Britain.

Fanny Westwood was another wife who religiously followed her husband around the country, staying in various digs and guest houses, until when heavily pregnant with their first child she decided not to risk the discomfiture of travel.

Even in these troubled times the Football League was determined to continue its War League programme. Both the Prime Minister and General Montgomery believed that the continuation of football was not only good for the morale of the nation, it also helped to keep life in perspective for the troops abroad. In one famous telegram received by the news agency Reuters from soldiers stationed in Malta, the plaintive request was transmitted, 'Please repeat Saturday football results – heavy bombing interfered with our reception'. Football, it seemed, was a welcome distraction from the most severe situations. To demonstrate his own resolve Winston Churchill once led six of his cabinet ministers to watch a match in the capital.

Although the 1940/41 season of football managed to get under way at the height of the Blitz it was possibly the most difficult of the wartime competitions. Due to the accepted hardships of raising eleven players, arranging fixtures and even securing venues that were not deemed to be in the target zone of German bombers, the Football League adopted many changes to the previous year's structure. Only 68 clubs elected to play this time around and they were simply divided into the North and South groups. Each club was responsible for selecting its own opponents, although each of the First and Second Division teams was also expected to complete fixtures against at least two Third Division teams. The clubs were then given a target to complete at least twenty games each, but no points would be awarded for any of these. Instead the final League table would be calculated solely on the goal average achieved by the competing teams. Had he known, Hitler may have seen this as a defiant challenge. To destroy the British spirit he must first destroy their national sport.

Watching the new season unfold was an envious Charles Foweraker, once again the unpaid manager of Bolton Wanderers Football Club. Despite the mounting complications now facing each club merely to participate in League football, Foweraker desperately wanted Bolton Wanderers to be involved. He still had his hard core of local players available to him, although without any home fixtures he would have to allow them to guest for any teams in the area that invited them to do so. Training sessions were still held whenever possible, especially to foster Foweraker's determination to encourage and maintain the enthusiasm among the new talent in his stable. Coach Walter Rowley was instructed to do his level best to keep the team, and the youth reserves, up to match fitness at all times. As this policy was vigorously pursued at Burnden Park Foweraker continually hounded the board of directors to allow them to rejoin the Football League. His argument was simple: without income of any sort the club clearly would not be able to continue in any form. Even the limited receipts from War League games would help to ensure their long-term survival.

Debate at board level continued until finally Charles Foweraker's wishes were granted, and Bolton Wanderers rejoined the League. It must be said that this was not a unanimous decision. Some directors still felt that total closure during wartime was the best option for the club. But the sway of the majority meant that on 4 January 1941 Oldham Athletic visited Burnden Park and the Football League North was back under way in Bolton. The Wanderers had been allowed to join the League at the halfway stage of the competition as the final positions table was to be calculated on goal average, and therefore their playing fewer matches than the other teams was of little or no consequence. A crowd of two thousand and thirty-eight witnessed the Oldham game, which was many times the number that had turned out seven months previously to watch those last matches played out under the shadow of the Dunkirk retreat.

Britain was still under nightly bombardment and the skies above the towns and cities were often dominated by fierce dogfights, but it is a measure of the British resolve at the time that the civilian population refused to bow to the aggressors. Life and sport would go on. Only the British weather could achieve what the Luftwaffe could not. In the depth of one of the worst winters on record several games between 25 January and 22 March had to be postponed or cancelled.

Right from their reintroduction into the League, team selection had been the bugbear for Charles Foweraker, especially in filling the right-half position. A guest, L. Martindale, had taken up this role for the opening two games, followed in the next two by Harry Goslin who was home on leave. A local player, Norman Hislop, wore the number four shirt next time out, but Foweraker was still not happy with the balance in his squad. Once again the manager turned to his youth development policy for inspiration and he was rewarded by the unearthing of a fresh, new and explosive talent. As the blackboard bearing the team line-ups was paraded around the Burnden Park perimeter track on 22 March 1941 there were gasps of surprise from the Bolton faithful. George Hunt, the regular centre-forward and top goal-scorer for the previous two seasons was being moved to the problem right-half position in order to accommodate a debutante by the name of Nat Lofthouse.

Many fans were aware that Nat had the reputation of being a good prospect for the future but they were all amazed at Foweraker's gamble on plunging him into first-team action so quickly. Charles Foweraker firmly believed Nat was up to the challenge, and Nat himself wanted to grasp this opportunity to establish his name. So at the age of fifteen years two hundred and seven days Nat Lofthouse lined up alongside several of his boyhood heroes to face Bury at Burnden Park. Foweraker's faith in his latest discovery was totally vindicated as young Nat scored two goals in their 5–1 victory that day. As an added bonus for the manager Lofthouse struck up an immediate rapport with Walter Sidebottom, his inside-forward, and the goals began to flow. In Nat's first six games for Bolton he and Walter Sidebottom scored ten goals between them and began a partnership that surely would have blossomed had the war not intervened.

Just as things were starting to take shape in Bolton's forward-line Walter Sidebottom was called up. Bolton had been prepared for this as he fell into the latest age qualification group to be set out by the government. Blackburn Rovers were the visitors to Burnden Park on 26 April 1941 and were beaten 2–0. Lofthouse and Sidebottom scored a goal a piece in what was to be Walter's last game before joining the Royal Navy to become a very active member of the armed forces. Nat Lofthouse, though, went from strength to strength. He played in all 11 games following his debut and ended the year with a haul of 11 goals.

Even as the waves of German planes continued to rain bombs and incendiaries on British cities and industrial heartlands throughout the spring of 1941 the games went on. Hardened to the horrors of the Blitz the crowds still turned out for their football, with an average of between fifteen hundred and two thousand attending the League matches at Burnden Park, and a War Cup game at home to Preston North End attracted close to 8,000 through the turnstiles. The only concession made by all the clubs to the aerial threat from the German air force was to engage 'spotters'. If the air-raid sirens went off during a match the game would not automatically be suspended, because to evacuate the ground of several thousand people needlessly would not only cause panic, it would also be difficult to co-ordinate and control. Only when the 'spotters' actually saw the bombers approaching would the referee be signalled to blow the whistle. Clearly the sport was a panacea and there was enough interest in the town to make football once again a viable proposition for the Wanderers.

Players received 30 shillings (£1.50) per game, with no bonuses for winning and no fee for training sessions. The only other costs for the home club were the sums of ten shillings and sixpence (52½p) for the referee and five shillings (25p) each for the linesmen, considerably higher wages than Ray Westwood and his fellow artillerymen were receiving for putting their necks on the line. Yet despite this apparently generous remuneration the recruitment of officials for the War League matches had been a problem throughout the whole of that season, so much so that in November 1940 the Football League changed its rules to allow referees wearing spectacles to control Regional League games, something which players, managers and spectators alike had been encouraging them to do since the Football League had begun!

On reflection the season, against all odds, had been a reasonably successful experiment for Bolton Wanderers. The board of directors was now in full agreement with Charles Foweraker about the future of the club, and resolved that football would continue to be played at Burnden Park throughout the duration of the war. For Nat Lofthouse life was getting better all the time. The 1941/42 season saw him play for the Bolton Wanderers first team on a further 12 occasions. He had responded to Foweraker's continued belief in him by scoring six times, to maintain the perfect centre-forward ratio of a goal in every other game. He was still, however, continuing his daytime employment at Peter Caffery and Sons, but both his colleagues and employers there were proud of Nat's growing football reputation and would encourage him all they could. Nat in his turn was pleased to be able to contribute to the family's income now that he was bringing in a regular wage. But what had really been on Nat's mind at the end of that season was his forthcoming 17th birthday. This was the age at which apprentice footballers could be offered a full-time professional contract, and Nat wanted one badly. His lifelong ambition had been to play for Bolton Wanderers. Having already made 23 first-team appearances and scored 17 goals Nat was optimistic about his chances. But he knew that the final decision would rest with Charles Foweraker, probably acting on the advice of the coach, Walter Rowley.

Charles Foweraker himself could look back on the 1941/42 season with a good deal of satisfaction. Despite the ongoing problems that the club had finding players the Wanderers had completed a 33-game League and Cup programme. Attendances had been averaging 2,000 to 3,000, with the highest gate of the year being 4,371 for their home game against Stoke City. Although there had been six players who had made over 20 appearances each over the course of the season the remaining places had been filled by a multitude of guests, youngsters and players home on leave, including seven of the Wartime Wanderers. All in all Bolton Wanderers had called upon the services of 62 different players throughout the year.

Foweraker was still convinced, however, that the best long-term prospects for the club lay in encouraging young talent; Nat Lofthouse was the jewel in the crown of the apprentice players and Foweraker was not about to let him slip through the net. Keeping a careful eye on the calendar Charles Foweraker invited Nat into his office at the first available opportunity following the boy's seventeenth birthday. In due course both their dreams were fulfilled. Nat Lofthouse was offered and accepted a full professional contract with Bolton Wanderers. The standard signing-on fee for all professional players was ten pounds, and as Nat signed his contract Charles Foweraker handed him two large white five-pound notes. Overjoyed, the young Nat ran straight home and proudly deposited the money on the kitchen table before his startled parents. At first his father queried where such an amount had come from, even considering the notion that Nat might have stolen it. After all, this was a full month's wages to Richard Lofthouse. As the realisation that their son could actually make a respectable living from playing football slowly sunk in, the doubting frowns were replaced by beaming smiles and proud congratulations. As an investment by Bolton Wanderers this transaction by Charles Foweraker must remain one of the shrewdest ever in the club's history.

Still in Bolton at this time was Territorial Army clerk Jimmy Gittens. Gittens was bored with his sedentary position and had applied for a posting overseas to see some active service. His wish was eventually granted when he was transferred to a clerical post with the 53rd Field Regiment Bolton Artillery, then stationed at barracks in Holt, Norfolk. Arriving at the camp the first person Jimmy Gittens saw was his old friend from Bolton, Ray Westwood. The two had been regular companions during Ray's midweek nights in Bolton and were often seen socialising together at the local Palais de Danse. Surprised to see his old mucker looking somewhat dishevelled in his crumpled army uniform Jimmy shouted over a greeting to attract Ray's attention. Ray's face lit up at seeing his long-time pal and they were soon reminiscing about their nights out on the town. But it rapidly dawned on Jimmy that there were more serious thoughts on Ray's mind. Fanny had given birth to their son Alan exactly a year before, and with the delivery her regular visits to see Ray had stopped. Ray was concerned that the child, whom he had seen only on two very brief occasions, needed his financial support. If Ray were to be able to remain in the country he would probably be able to start guesting. The fee for one match alone would be more than the army paid him in a fortnight. Ray was desperate to avoid an overseas posting.

On his first day in the clerical office at Holt Jimmy Gittens looked up from his desk to see Ray approaching purposefully. Jimmy asked his friend where he was going and was told, 'To see the MO.' Gittens was aware of the rumours about the foreign destination of the Regiment and queried whether the purpose of Ray's visit was to equip himself with anti-malaria tablets and mosquito repellent.

'They'll not be sending me anywhere,' retorted Ray, 'I've got an appointment due at Peterborough Hospital to have a cartilage operation on my knee.'

Every day before the Regiment was due to embark this routine was repeated, until on the actual day of their shipment the realisation dawned on Ray that the appointment was not going to arrive in time. Ray stormed from the office cursing the Army: 'I'll sue them. I'll sue them for every ruddy penny they've got.'

On 15 July 1942 the 53rd Field Regiment RA responded to the

orders to mobilise for overseas service that had been received on 2 June and journeyed to their port of embarkation. Extra men had been drafted in from other units to bring the numbers up to war establishment levels. The necessary preparations duly completed, the unit set sail for the Middle East where they would have to contend with both the enemy and the hostile climatic conditions.

Just a day after the fleet had departed a clerk at Holt received a telegram addressed to the 53rd Field Regiment RA for the attention of Gunner Westwood R. The terse message read, 'Gunner Ray Westwood report to Peterborough Hospital'. Not knowing if this message carried any cryptic significance or not the clerk decided to relay it to Jimmy Gittens on board the troop ship.

SIX

Jimmy Gittens was on duty as a clerk in the radio room aboard the troop-ship bound for the Middle East when the telegram finally caught up with them. They had been in port for two days prior to embarkation on 17 July yet it had failed to arrive. When it did land on the clerk's desk in the port office at Gourock there was the usual SNAFU as no one could say with any degree of certainty which vessel Ray Westwood had actually sailed on. In keeping with the saga to date the message was then bounced around the fleet for the next seven days. With no possibility of responding to the hospital appointment in the affirmative Jimmy decided to pocket the scrap of paper bearing the evidence that could have cancelled Ray's posting. At an appropriate time in the future, when it would have the most emotional impact, Jimmy would deliver the obsolete telegram.

Three days later they called in for supplies at Freetown, the port capital of Sierra Leone on the west coast of Africa. It would have been suicide to attempt to run the gauntlet of the Mediterranean between Nazi-occupied Europe and the heavy concentration of German and Italian forces building up along the entire North African coastline. With the majority of the islands also under the imposed rule of the Axis powers the enemy had further ensured their dominance in the air. The strain of the long sea voyage, in seriously overcrowded conditions, became virtually insupportable when they received orders that no one, other than a few senior officers, would be allowed shore leave. Still Jimmy decided to refrain from being the harbinger of bad tidings.

There were few ships in the British fleet that would have been specifically designed to carry the numbers that were now required of them. Some were refitted cruise ships with peacetime accommodation for 200, now transporting upwards of 2,000 soldiers each. This necessitated equipping the holds with rows of three-tier bunks. Even the NCOs, who were assigned the luxury of a single cabin, found themselves sharing with eight others. If they were lucky they may have found some solace in the provision of the occasional glass of beer. Those aboard the American ships, now in Allied service, would have been subjected to a self-imposed prohibition. On-deck conditions would have been equally cramped, although attempts to maintain a daily regime of physical exercise would have been fulfilled, even to the point of organising competitive events, such as boxing matches and tug-of-war tournaments. Some ships' companies managed to stage complete sports days. These, and other activities, music concerts, debating societies, even the publishing of a daily newspaper such as *The Ocean News,* as happened on the SS *Santa Rosa* – fortunate enough to number among its passengers Lieutenant Hugh Cudlipp, later Lord Cudlipp, a former editor with the *Sunday Pictorial* and the *Daily Mirror* who was to become head of the Mirror Group – were largely organised by the men themselves. Proposals would have been put to the individual company commanders, with the ultimate decision resting with the OC (Officer Commanding Troops at Sea). This rank was often filled by very senior career officers who were felt to be too old for active service. Indeed, some of them were actually brought out of retirement to perform these duties.

Five days of looking at terra firma without the permission to set foot on it must have been a testing experience. So it would have been with some relief that shortly after setting sail on 1 August the troops were allowed to let their hair down in a riotous 'Crossing-the-Line' ceremony. This traditional, yet unorthodox, celebration to mark the passage from the northern to the southern hemisphere via the Equator requires the participants to make sacrifices to King Neptune, god of the sea. Ernie Forrest would no doubt have been in his element, participating in the costumed antics and tossing his companions into a makeshift pool set up on the decks. For Ray, too, it would have offered a brief moment of escapism that even Jimmy and his telegram would not deny him.

Arriving in Cape Town, the mid-point of their two-month-long journey, the Bolton Wanderers were to be temporarily reminded of their celebrity status when they were met by a reception committee of local dignitaries headed by the British High Commissioner, with an invitation for the entire team to be house guests at Government House. For Lieutenant Goslin this was a formal request his rank could not refuse, but special dispensation would have to be granted to release the other players into his cognisance, and Ernie could have been a liability.

His antics were never malicious but they were always mischievous, and his cutting satire was often just too close to the truth. This combination of intelligence and free spirit had already seen him promoted to sergeant, and broken back to private almost before the stripes had been sewn on. Ernie was an essential ingredient for a good party, without which Ray, Stan, Donny and most of the others would not have partaken.

Slightly the worse for wear after a good evening they made it back to the ship with only moments to spare before the convoy set sail. There were several soldiers on this and other ships that never did make it, either through accident or design. For the majority that did it was to be another month of ocean-going tedium, with just a brief respite to take on fresh water at Aden, the gateway to the Red Sea. Here they parted company with their destroyer escort for the last leg of their journey to Port Tewfik, the southern entrance to the Suez Canal, their only protection a barrage balloon strung out from the stern on a windlass.

The day the 53rd set foot on Egyptian soil, the infantry and armoured brigades to which they were ultimately to provide artillery support to were deeply embroiled in the Battle of Alam Halfa, an action that could be deemed a precursor to the famous El Alamein. Shortly after midnight on 30 August the enemy had launched an assault on the Allies' main defensive position in the Western Desert. Having penetrated the minefields the 15th and 21st Panzer Divisions forced back the British 7th Armoured Division towards the Alam Halfa ridge where a major tank battle was to ensue. For two whole days the entire area was to be subjected to dive-bombing by Stukas, artillery shelling and ricochets from the anti-tank guns before the Desert Air Force and the New Zealand Division joined the counter offensive, successfully pushing the enemy back to the original front.

The heavy losses sustained by both sides brought about a temporary lull in the fighting as each reorganised and resupplied. Unwilling to commit their full forces at this time the British High Command had kept the Bolton Artillery out of this action. Bivouacked at Camp 32, Tahag, close to their point of disembarkation, they were to be extensively drilled in desert warfare, exercises and training that were to continue at the most forward base, Cowley Camp, in an area designated the New Zealand Box. It was to be here on the night of 11 October 1942 that the Regiment was to fire its first rounds in the new theatre of war.

As the bulk of the 53rd were pulling out of Tahag destined for that front line Jimmy Gittens had caught sight of Ray Westwood, leaning against his new staff car. Ray had requested, and been granted, permission to be temporarily transferred to his brother's unit now stationed at Alexandria on the Mediterranean coast. To his great relief this would take him in the opposite direction to the hostilities. Jimmy smiled as he produced the well travelled telegram: 'This arrived for you the day we left Norfolk. Missed you by that much,' he gestured with his thumb and forefinger, 'and the Adjutant didn't think it important enough to chase after you.' Jimmy slammed his foot on the accelerator of his own military vehicle to escape the expected violent reaction. Looking in the rear view mirror he witnessed Ray brandishing his rifle and loudly threatening to shoot the Adjutant.

If Ray had thought a posting to Alexandria would keep him out of the action he was to be sadly disappointed. The British fleet that had arrived in the Mediterranean either via the Suez Canal or by surviving the convoy route from Gibraltar with submarine support, was now helplessly penned in the harbour. Ray watched in horror from the safety of his trench as the Stukas launched their aerial bombardment. Shore batteries joined the ship-mounted guns in a violent retaliation, while Ray kept his head down and seriously began composing what he thought would be his first and last letter home from the Middle East.

Montgomery and his fellow officers had already conceived the battle plan for El Alamein and set a commencement date of 23 October. In the run-up to the appointed hour reinforcements and new equipment for all the armed services continued to arrive, including the first contingent of 300 American Sherman tanks. By the time the offensive was to open the Allies not only had achieved a clear air superiority, they also outnumbered the German troops and tanks by more than two to one.

In the days leading up to this operation Harry Goslin and his men were deployed preparing dummy positions in a segment known as the Oxford Gap. In order to draw enemy fire fake gun emplacements, canvas tanks and truck carcasses were strategically distributed in areas adjacent to where their actual positions were to be located. The dumping of 430 rounds of ammunition per gun also took place in those last 24 hours. On the night of 22 October the 53rd Field Regiment of the Bolton Artillery occupied its battle position. At 2200 hours on the 23rd the Battle of El Alamein commenced with a hurricane of artillery bombardment along the entire front line. Twenty minutes into the action the 1st and 10th Armoured Divisions began a two-lane penetration of the enemy lines. By 0405 hours on that first morning of the offensive that was ultimately to decide the outcome of the war in North Africa the commanders were able to report back to General HQ, 'Advancing on all fronts'. The Germans committed their entire 15th Panzer Division to containing this break-in, but already the Allies were manoeuvring to outflank them. The Allied superiority also enabled them to repel the strong enemy resistance in the south even though many of the troops were being sent north towards the coast where a bitter dogfight was developing. The defence of this coastal corridor, on which the Allies depended for effective communication, was vital. On 25 October the 53rd were also moved in this direction to repel a diversionary attack the Axis powers were mounting from Kidney Hill, just west of the emerging front line, Miteiriya Ridge, which the Allies codenamed the Springbok Track.

Over the ensuing days this commanding position, midway between the coast and the Qattara Depression which formed the southern boundary of the battlefield, was to become the Allies' prime objective. The Bolton Artillery dropped down to Ruweisat Ridge to plug any gaps that might appear in the front line as a result of Rommel's resourceful use of his remaining Panzer divisions. On 1 November another heavy artillery barrage was launched against a beleaguered enemy, followed by a bitter tank battle that within 24 hours was to reduce the German armour to just 35 serviceable tanks.

Field Marshal Erwin Rommel, overall commander of the Afrika Korps, decided to withdraw, an order that Hitler countermanded. But it was too late. The Allied troops had already broken the German lines and their armour was pouring through, forcing the remnants of Rommel's army into a full retreat westwards along the coast towards Tobruk. Harry Goslin and the 53rd Field Regiment joined the pursuit, a devastating rout that was to be temporarily hampered by heavy rains on 7 November turning the once baked desert into a veritable quagmire.

Ray Westwood had been transferred back into the unit around the time of El Alamein but only after he had been admitted to the military hospital in Alexandria where the army surgeon had performed the necessary cartilage operation. This ongoing knee injury had kept Ray out of a great deal of football since he joined the forces, so now it was hoped his good form on the field would return. But these minor operations and illnesses were something that were to recur throughout the remainder of Ray's army career, successfully keeping him out of harm's way for much of the duration of the hostilities. He made no excuses about the fact that he had no stomach for fire fights, but there were valuable support roles he could, and would, play. He was still the CO's driver, and to perfect his skills he had volunteered for a mechanics course, which he duly completed while convalescing in Cairo. There are no witnesses that have yet come forward to verify that he ever had a tool in his hand, either while in service or in civvy street; in fact no one can recall Ray ever performing any manual task, as he chose to limit his physical exertions to the football pitch.

Ray's only son, Alan, whom Ray had rarely seen before he left for the Middle East was now a toddler trying to mouth his first words. But Fanny had heard no word at all from her husband since well before his embarkation. There had been no official telegram from the War Office either, so she assumed with relief that he had not been killed or reported missing in action. However, feeling the need to be more self-sufficient, and probably missing the extra money from the first instalment of the Bolton Wanderers benefit payment when Ray was in England, Fanny had decided to go back to work. She was still living with her in-laws, so having someone to take care of baby Alan was not a problem, and certainly at this time there was no shortage of work for women. The thought had barely begun to take root, let alone evolve into concrete action, before she received the first letter from Ray in almost a year. It was brief, and the tone somewhat chauvinistic. He informed Fanny that he had recently passed a mechanics course which entitled him to additional pay. 'But you'll receive none of it,' he asserted, 'if you insist on returning to work, as I have been reliably informed is your intention.' To this day Fanny has no idea how he found out. But she was pleased that it had solicited such a rapid response, if for no other reason than to confirm that he was alive and well.

Nearly three months into the new football calendar and Nat Lofthouse was continuing where he left off the previous season as one of Bolton's more prolific goal-scorers. This was partly due to the fact that he was one of only a handful of regular players. The joint effect of the continuing army recruitment and the guesting system had meant that the club was obliged virtually to double the roll-call of players who would appear throughout the season, compared to the 22 full timers signed to the Wanderers at the outbreak of war. However, this combination of youthful inexperience and the inability to play a regular team, who would have had an opportunity to train together more frequently, was having an effect on their overall performance and the Olympian's prediction made during the first year of war was being tragically fulfilled. Despite the supreme efforts of Nat and his largely teenage team-mates the Wanderers lost seven of their first ten matches, which kept them at the bottom of the League, and in peacetime would have assured their relegation. But Nat was undeterred. His ambitions were being played out on the pitch, and after the game another passion was blooming.

Nat had always harboured an affection for Alma Foster, ever since their days together at Castle Hill School. As a shy schoolboy he had never had the courage to talk to her. Now with his improved stature, and the confidence he had gained from a full season as a regular member of the first team, his first reunion with Alma since leaving school was to reveal another new and positive trait to his character. One weekday afternoon he was down at Trinity Street railway station saying farewell to the latest member of the Wanderers' squad to be posted abroad as an army volunteer when he caught a glimpse of Alma further down the platform. She, too, was seeing a soldier off, and for a moment Nat's heart fell. But as the train pulled away and the crowds thinned he plucked up the nerve to approach her. Alma was already well ahead of him and mounting the stairs that would take her over the platform bridge and out into the busy town centre. As he sprinted after her his mind focused sufficiently to admire her legs. Eventually drawing alongside her he was somewhat out of breath, a condition that only added to his embarrassment as he fumbled for words. In the brief passage of time before they emerged into the street Nat had been able to ascertain that Alma was now a hairdresser, the soldier was just a friend and she would be at the Empress Dance Hall that Saturday night. Nat was beaming.

Ray Westwood had many fond memories of his own nights at the Empress, but now encamped dangerously near the front line that is all they were. He had recovered from his latest operation and was likely to be sent into action when a fortuitous chance to indulge his own passion came his way. Early in 1942, with the announcement of a General Election in Egypt, King Farouk had given cause for the Allies to question his allegiance, and whether he may even be considering breaking the treaty they had signed as early as 1936. This scenario gained some credence due to the fact that the Egyptian Prime Minister of the time was believed to be a German sympathiser. There were those within the British intelligence service who had even considered meddling in Egypt's internal affairs to ensure that a more pliable incumbent was returned to this high office. Fortuitously the victor at the polls was to be one Mustafa An-Nahhas, leader of the pro-British Wafd party.

Not wishing to let politics interfere with historical events the military hierarchy desperately needed to have a public relations coup to further endorse their victories on the battlefield, and to put Egypt firmly in her place. It was known that the King's education in England had endeared him to the national sport. On his return to Cairo he had built up what he believed to be an invincible 11 at his home ground, the National Sporting Club, sited in the exclusive Cairo suburb of Gezira Island, a verdant oasis in the midst of the horrors of war. As Jack Roberts recalls, 'it was very much a high level initiative' that saw the British Army bring their best football team to this pristine stadium for a challenge match against King Farouk's national side. The Allies' own invincible 11 was to comprise no fewer than ten Bolton Wanderers first-team players, and the ersatz Trotter, Billy Ainscow.

Tommy Woodward cannot remember how he came to be selected for this team. Although he had been at Burnden Park since he was a 17 year-old apprentice secured from the Westhoughton Club, White Horse Temperance, his pre-war play was confined to sharing the wing role with the then more experienced Albert Geldard, who unbeknown to Tommy at that time had not joined the 53rd in North Africa; instead he had remained in the UK as a physical training instructor. What is more, when the other players had volunteered for the army in 1939 Tommy had chosen the RAF, and had been serving as a medic in the Middle East since the Allies first established themselves in the region during August 1940, following the build-up of Italian forces in Libya, Ethiopia, Eritrea and Italian Somaliland which had made them the largest combatant group in North Africa. After three months in the battle lines of the Western Desert Tommy and his unit were pulled back to the relatively safe haven of Cairo, so he had already been encamped at the Cairo headquarters for close to two years when he was to be briefly reunited with his old squad from the Bolton turf. Tommy remembers well the day he ran into Harry Goslin and the lads from Burnden Park. They had not met since the outbreak of war, and although he had heard of Harry's promotion to Lieutenant he was not surprised to find that officer status had not changed him. He and his battery had literally only just returned, battle-weary and grimy, from the front line. But ready to play football.

Jack Hurst was actually on a gun, firing, when he received his orders to return to Cairo, a clear indication of how important this event was rated by the senior commanders. While Jack tried to feign surprise at this request, his comrades in 209 Battery were becoming accustomed to his special dispensation to play football. The one constant item in

Jack's kitbag, no matter where they were, what action they were involved in, was a cleaned pair of football boots.

For Ernie Forrest complying with the order to travel was fraught with danger. If he thought finding his way through wartime France, without lights and with the absence of directional signs, was difficult then navigating across a sea of featureless sand was virtually impossible. He was in a Quad with an officer and four other soldiers, with a deadline to be in Cairo, when they found themselves confronted by a minefield. Whether it was one of ours or one of theirs even the officer was not prepared to say with any degree of certainty. The entire area had been criss-crossed by the Germans, Italians and the Allies for months, with each side adding to the lethal trap. Ernie leapt defiantly from the vehicle with the declaration, 'If we go through there I'll get me bloody legs blown off. I'll end me career playing football with stumps.' If they were to have any chance of arriving in Cairo at their appointed hour they had no alternative. Despite his protestations Ernie jumped back into the vehicle and headed out across the minefield, the officer out in front as a sweeper.

The facilities at the National Sporting Club put Burnden Park to shame. For the first time since their posting to North Africa the players would be able to indulge in the luxury of running water. The newly installed showers had barely been christened before the hostilities brought a temporary halt to the regular fixtures on Gezira Island. But on this occasion it was almost as if the armistice had already been signed. The main covered stand was replete with King Farouk's entourage and a full contingent of British military brass. On the sand and stone terraces surrounding the pitch the highly charged local supporters mingled with an army of non-combatant and injured Allies, together with those soldiers currently on 48-hour leave from the front line. The roar that lifted up from the crowd as the teams emerged was almost reminiscent of the pre-war days on the Wanderers' home ground, a truly rousing reception that was all the more euphoric because Ernie Forrest and his passengers had arrived in their battered Quad just moments before kick-off.

The ensuing game had all the thrills and excitement of a cup-tie. For Goslin's team it was a release of tension. This was their first respite from action in over a month. Thirty days of living on the edge. Several comrades were now dead. Some were reported missing in action. But miraculously the Bolton Wanderers were still intact. The loyalty and spirit that had been forged in their many years together that had tragically culminated with that declaration on 3 September 1939 had now become a totally impenetrable bond. There were those who said, 'Never take on a Wanderer, because if you kick one of them, you kick them all, and you'll then have to be prepared to take on the whole team.' An epithet that King Farouk's eleven were to help prove to their detriment.

There was an extra free ration of beer for the victorious players that evening, and Stan Hanson was to be the first to the mess bar to receive it. Many had tried, but none had succeeded in beating this Wanderers' goalkeeper in a race for a pint of best bitter. It was one of those occasions when Harry Goslin would allow them that extra rope with which to immerse themselves in a night of raucous revelry. Only Jack Hurst was to abstain, but then he always had been abstemious. Even the loss of his only son and three years of bitter war had not broken his will. His one regret was that he felt unable to fully express himself in his letters home because of the censorship. In this brief moment together before being returned to their separate front-line positions Harry Goslin extended his officer's privilege to his friend of long standing, and guaranteed to forward Jack's latest missive to Betty unopened.

That was the last Tommy Woodward was to see of the Wanderers until the war was over. Their all too brief leave expressly to meet that challenge from the Egyptian national football team was over and it was back to the front line for Harry Goslin and his squad.

Even as the church bells were being rung in celebration of the Allies' victorious move into Libya preparations were being made against a counter attack. Despite the enemy now surrendering daily in droves, and the 53rd Regiment's unopposed entry into Tobruk, this was not a time to be lackadaisical. Harry Goslin's unit had made camp in a wadi beyond the city perimeter as they awaited orders for the next stage of the push. The two opposing armies were now following almost parallel tracks along the coastline with the barest strip of no-man's-land between them. As the battery dug in for the night Harry posted Jimmy Gittens and Ernie Forrest as sentries on the northernmost sand ridge. With a great amount of cursing and extreme physical exertion they eventually succeeded in dragging a Bren gun, still in its armoured casing, and what appeared to them to be an unnecessarily large amount of ammunition up onto their appointed guard position. As they collapsed onto the rapidly cooling sand and looked seaward they were surprised, and not a little worried, to spot what they perceived to be a circle of enemy vehicles bedded in for the night away on the horizon. In desperation they prepared to mount their defence. But the armoured casing was jammed. After several futile attempts at releasing the catches that would enable them to retrieve the Bren gun from within, they surrendered to the inevitable.

'Not that it would be any good if we did get it out,' muttered Jimmy. 'I've never been able to work one of those ruddy guns anyway.'

'Me neither,' Ernie sighed, as he resigned himself to spending the entire night with his eyes trained on the distant enemy camp for the slightest sign of movement. 'I think I had a match the day they did the Bren gun course.'

At first light it was apparent that the vehicles had been abandoned and the troops long since surrendered. What still survived of Rommel's Afrika Korps was already further west, heading for Tunisia, and keeping a safe distance between themselves and Montgomery's forces, whose hot pursuit was being spearheaded by the 7th Armoured Division. Although the Germans had not been as decisively beaten as the Allied High Command had planned, the Western Desert was now virtually cleared. The armoured divisions would maintain the pursuit well into the New Year, when the final stragglers of Rommel's army would be forced to surrender in Algeria and Morocco, surrounded by Allied troops and the sometimes less than co-operative French North African Garrison. The only possible avenue of retreat for the enemy was the Mediterranean and this was by that time securely under the control of the British and American combined fleets. So by the end of November 1942 the support of the artillery was no longer required and the 53rd was ordered to return to Cairo where they would be granted 48 hours' leave, enabling refitting to proceed prior to being moved to PAIFORCE (Persian and Iraq Force).

British forces had been occupying Iraq since May 1941, following an army coup in which a pro-German faction had seized power. In conjunction with the Russians the British had also occupied Persia in August of that year. This was because of the obvious pro-German sympathies of the Shah, demonstrated by the large number of German advisers he had encouraged to become established in Tehran. During 1942 the stability of the area had been further threatened by the rapid German advance into Russia, during which some units had reached as far as the Caucasus Mountains from where they had relatively easy access into Iran either via the Caspian Sea or the southern Soviet-occupied republics of Georgia, Azerbaijan and Armenia. Given their recent history these three states that had been forced into the Transcaucasian Republic might even have been deemed more sympathetic to the invading forces.

It was against this backdrop that Harry Goslin and his men descended on Cairo on Christmas Eve 1942. Word must have filtered through about the Nazi's planned winter offensive that could see the German Army pressing dangerously close to the Persian frontier. If Hitler's forces were to succeed in penetrating into this oil-rich region then the 53rd Bolton Artillery would most certainly be in the thick of the heavy fighting once again.

They needed an escape. Apart from the evening entertainment in the form of concerts and vaudeville-style shows, there were the inevitable football matches. By this time there were some 300 teams throughout the Middle East organised in various divisions, each with their own League table and cup tournament. The logistics required to co-ordinate and stage manage these events were on a par with those employed to direct the course of the war. For the clerks and quartermasters who were generally at the hub of this activity it was their own personal form of rest and recreation. But for Ernie Forrest the entire competition needed something of a twist.

In the brief time he had available Ernie succeeded in arranging a match against the German and Italian PoWs. Officially this never took place, as it could have been seen as fraternising with the enemy, and thereby warrant a court-martial. Those who participated saw it as a peace initiative in the season of goodwill. No doubt Ernie took the inspiration from that famous international between British and German soldiers that reportedly took place on another Christmas Day on the battlefields of the Somme during the First World War.

The Bolton Wanderers regular team were probably having a far worse time in their own perception of things. Nat had persuaded Alma and some of the other wives and girlfriends to accompany him and the Wanderers on 25 December for the short journey to Manchester United's wartime ground. Despite not having had a win since October Nat was still the top scorer of the season. Now buoyed by the festive spirit they were hoping to seek recompense for the 2–0 victory United had secured at Burnden Park just the week before. Unfortunately it was not to be. The less experienced Trotters, with their youthful contingent, were to suffer a humiliating 4–0 defeat at the feet of a full professional team that had changed little since the last full season before the war. In that year Goslin's team had held them to a draw on both legs of the League tournament.

On New Year's Eve, as Nat was making his own resolutions in the hope that they would help his club achieve better results in the remaining 1943 portion of the season, the away team, still under the

stalwart leadership of Harry Goslin, was crossing the Jordan Valley to
the Mafraq staging post, from where it was to be a gruelling five-day
journey to Baghdad.

SEVEN

From Baghdad the Regiment moved on to Kirkurk, arriving there on 8 January 1943. The 53rd Field Regiment had now joined the 8th Indian Division and was affiliated to the 19th Brigade under the command of Brigadier T.S. Dobree, who himself had recently been transferred from the 6th Indian. After only a very short stay at Kirkurk the Wartime Wanderers were relocated to Kifri in Iraq, which was to become their main base for the next five months.

Kifri held great strategic importance in the Middle East war. The region of Persia directly to the north that had been threatened by the rapid German advance had been removed from immediate danger by a successful Russian counter attack during the winter months. By February 1943 the German Sixth Army had capitulated at Stalingrad, and although this effectively ended the direct military threat to Persia and Iraq the Allies felt it necessary to maintain a strong army presence in the region. The Wartime Wanderers' duties in Kifri and the surrounding areas were to preserve internal security, to protect the oil installations and pipelines, and to keep open the overland supply route for American equipment to be shipped from the Persian Gulf to Russia.

Kifri is a small town situated midway between Khanaqin and Kirkurk. The town's military significance lay in the fact that it was close to the road and railway lines running north from Baghdad. The main feature of Kifri that the British troops had to contend with was the intense heat from the unrelenting sunshine. Daytime temperatures reached one hundred and twenty-one degrees Fahrenheit in the shade, which severely restricted the amount of training and manoeuvres that could be done; training was therefore carried out in the hours before 10 a.m. and after 5 p.m. each day in order to escape the worst of the heat. Just to occupy the men various specialist instruction and training courses were held daily under canvas, but this still left the soldiers with considerable spare time on their hands.

Ernie Forrest and Ray Westwood lost no time in inventing new games which would not only while away the hours but would also be suitable for them to run a book on, and thereby indulge their passion for gambling. One favourite was to surround a scorpion with a ring of fire and let their comrades bet on whether or not the cornered arachnid would escape. When thus trapped a scorpion will either attempt to run through the flames and risk death, or turn its sting on itself and commit suicide. Who knows how the odds were calculated, but Forrest and Westwood reputedly earned enough to get by.

But daily life was by no means easy for the men. The excessive heat also meant a shortage of water, especially for ablutions. Often five or six men would have to wash from the same bucket, one after another. The burning sunshine, the insects which were everywhere and this lack of any proper hygiene facilities combined to create serious health risks. By February Billy Ainscow was one of the first to succumb to these conditions and was bedridden for ten days suffering from acute dysentery. All manner of tropical diseases were rife in the desert and the army hospitals were soon overflowing with troops not wounded in action but victims of the climate and conditions.

Despite all the harsh realities of desert warfare the Wartime Wanderers' spirit could not be broken. As usual, when the chips were down, out came the football to bring relief from the stress of military life. Incredibly a regular feature of their desert existence became the afternoon football match kicking off at 2 p.m. with the temperature on the exposed pitch nudging 125 degrees Fahrenheit. The players soon became known as the 'Mad Dogs' because of these forays under the blistering sun. But they earned the admiration and respect of those who could only watch and marvel at their fitness and strength of character. Word soon got around about the 'mad dog' footballers and they became a talking point for the Allied troops. One of these conversations led to a claim from some Iraqi soldiers that they had a team that could more than match the Wartime Wanderers and a challenge was thrown down. Wheels of organisation were put into motion and very soon the game was on. Permission to play had been sought through the appropriate chain of command and eventually the participation of the men under his command was readily sanctioned by Major Greenhalgh. It was agreed that this Iraqi team should visit the army base and a pitch was hurriedly prepared. Of course there was no grass so the game had to be played on the sharp desert sand. Two uprights were positioned at either end of the field of play whose lines had been simply scratched into the desert.

When the Iraqi players arrived on the appointed day it soon became apparent that they did not either possess or intend to play in any kind of sports footwear. In what many may have construed a bravado display of brinkmanship they claimed they were used to playing barefoot and that was how they intended to play this game. Harry Goslin called his men into a huddle. Clearly if the Wanderers players were to wear their heavy boots they could inflict serious injury when tackling their opponents; not an unfair advantage in Ernie's book, but perhaps not sportsmanlike. The British agreed also to play barefoot. The 'mad dogs' had really excelled themselves this time. The watching soldiers looked on in amazement as the Bolton Wanderers, including Billy Ainscow just recovering from his bout of dysentery, took to the pitch in perpetual motion in order to limit static contact between bare feet and scorching sand. Their baggy khaki flapped wildly as they responded to the opening whistle. The conditions could not have been any further removed from those at Burnden Park on a wet Saturday in November, but the Bolton players delighted their capacity crowd with another glorious victory.

News of the Wartime Wanderers' latest exploits travelled fast. Soon a new challenge was thrown at them, this time from a team of hard-bitten Polish troops who were calling themselves the champions of Persia and Iraq. National pride was now at stake and the game took on huge importance for the British army. To combat the Poles a group of very senior British officers was entrusted with putting together the best possible team they could muster from the thousands of British troops serving in Persia and Iraq, to be called the Paiforce XI. The new Commander in Chief of the Persia and Iraq Force, Lieutenant General Sir Henry Pownall, set up a trial game between the 'probables' and the 'possibles' in order to make a final team selection. In the 'probables' side there were seven Wanderers: Stan Hanson, Val Thompson, Harry Goslin, Jack Hurst, Ernie Forrest, Donny Howe and George Catterall. A hat-trick from Donny Howe contributed to the probables 5–1 victory, a win that may have been even more emphatic had Ray Westwood not been sidelined by another knee injury.

With the Paiforce XI confirmed the British army organised the game to take place at the Scouts Ground in Baghdad. Harry Goslin was invited to captain the side and four of his team-mates – Hanson, Howe, Forrest and Catterall – travelled by army truck to play in the game with him. By now the match was the talk of the Middle East and the Wartime Wanderers were amazed at the scenes in Baghdad. A crowd of 9,000 had assembled at the stadium, complete with football rattles, whistles and flags. The most senior Allied personnel rubbed shoulders with the leading military and diplomatic figures of Persia and Iraq to watch the spectacle of the British army versus the Polish army.

The crowd were to enjoy a thrilling game executed at an intense pace by the European players in the most extreme heat. The Paiforce XI took a first-minute lead when an early corner was forced home. Stan Hanson, however, could do nothing to prevent the equaliser that came from a penalty in the 34th minute. Right on half-time the Polish gained a 2–1 advantage as their mounting pressure on the British defence finally forced a second goal in the 44th minute. Harry Goslin was not to be beaten. An inspired half-time talk to his players produced a battling second half performance. Ernie Forrest was working terrifically in midfield and pounced on a half chance to equalise for the British after thirty five minutes. Thirteen minutes later, Moss, an amateur army player, scored a third, and two minutes from time the Wanderers' Donny Howe drove home a penalty to secure the result. The British tommies in the crowd were ecstatic. There could now be no doubt that the British army were the champions of Persia and Iraq. The five Wartime Wanderers who had been so influential in this victory returned triumphant to the 53rd Field Regiment's camp. In the entire 11 no other unit or professional club had been represented by more than one player. Another piece of history had been written for the Bolton Artillery and Bolton Wanderers.

Their status as footballers may have improved but their living conditions certainly had not. There would be little opportunity to bask in glory as they returned to the extreme physical hardship of desert life. Sleeping was often difficult, not to say impossible. The army had provided tents for their accommodation but these were often in short supply. Some of the Wanderers' players were having to use the canvas cover of a 180-pound gun as a makeshift shelter. During the night the air beneath this heavy canvas would get unbearably hot and stifling. The men would often dig deep into the sand in order to find somewhere relatively cool to sleep. Eventually the ground level inside these improvised tents would be some four feet lower than that outside.

As an officer Harry Goslin enjoyed a little more comfort than his team-mates, yet typically he would often share these benefits with them. Jack Hurst once received a call from Goslin to report to his quarters. On arrival Hurst was ushered into the Lieutenant's tent, then out through the rear flap where Goslin had instructed his batman to hang up a large bucket with irregular holes pierced in the bottom. Harry Goslin personally filled this bucket with water for his friend Jack Hurst to enjoy the regal luxury of a cold shower as a brief respite from the heat and grime of Kifri.

At home the 1942/43 football season had kicked off amid a general air of optimism. The air-raids not only seemed a thing of the past, they were about to be turned full circle on to the Nazis themselves following Air Marshal Sir Arthur 'Bomber' Harris's promise to 'scourge the Third Reich from end to end', with devastating air-raids 'every night and every day rain, blow or snow'. Even news from the front line was steadily improving as the year wore on, to the point that the Football League committee commenced discussions on how they would organise the first post-war season following the cessation of hostilities. By mid-season Nat had found his scoring touch and the crowds began to increase as word got around that Bolton Wanderers were playing some better football.

Off the pitch Alma Foster had become Nat's steady girlfriend, and hardly a weekend went by without their being seen around the town together, either at the cinemas or dancing the night away at the Empress or the Palais.

Results for the Wanderers were still patchy, however, and once again this can partly be put down to team selection problems in which heavy use of the guesting system was still a prominent feature. But this season was to see three guests in particular who were to have a lasting impact on the football world. Early in the season Foweraker had managed to secure the services of a young Preston North End winger who was just starting to make a name for himself. On that occasion Tom Finney helped the Wanderers secure their first away win of the season. Although it was Nat Lofthouse who actually scored both of the winning goals the two players had quickly developed an understanding that would come to fruition much later in their careers while wearing the white shirts of the English national squad. The two Lancastrians had started a friendship that has lasted throughout their lives, and taken them quite literally all over the world in the name of sport.

As well as being on Motherwell's books as an amateur wing-half Matt Gillies was a medical student in Glasgow before war broke out. Serving as an RAF navigator he was stationed at Blackpool at the beginning of the 1942/43 season, and it was in a match against that town's team that he was first selected to play for Bolton Wanderers. A fortuitous finding for the club, he not only signed professional papers with them at the end of the war but actually went on to captain the team in 1946/47. Later in his career he would manage Leicester City and Nottingham Forest, a far cry from the life he would have had if he had pursued his studies to become a doctor.

Willie Moir, a Scot from Bucksburn in Aberdeenshire who had developed in junior football in the Lossiemouth area, was also in the RAF, but stationed at Kirham. Billeted with him was Charlton Athletic's wing-half, Bert Johnson, who had already played as a guest for Bolton Wanderers on numerous occasions. In all Johnson was to play 100 games for the Wanderers before the RAF transferred him to quarters near Lincoln in Derbyshire, from where he was to pay a moving tribute to his former hosts in an open letter to the *Bolton Evening News*, presumably written with the Waterman fountain pen presented to him by the Wanderers manager on his departure: 'The friendships I have made in Bolton, and in the club itself will always bring happy memories. I don't think I could have been better treated anywhere than at Burnden Park.' Having seen Moir play for the Kirham station team Bert Johnson had recommended him to Bolton's chief scout, Bob Jackson. Moir's Commanding Officer was persuaded to allow Willie to have time off to play a trial match. In April 1943 Willie Moir signed as an amateur, but such was the early impression he made that the club offered him a professional contract three weeks later.

Although the signing of new young players was still very much a Charles Foweraker initiative a good deal of the day-to-day running of the club was now being handled by his number two, Walter Rowley. Foweraker was not in good health, and there were those among the directors who believed that a change of management was long overdue. It was not that Foweraker was doing a bad job, in fact the directors were unanimously impressed with the new talent he was bringing into the club; but there was a growing optimism that the war may soon be over. This would mean the return of the older pre-war players and the club was heading for a conflict. Many of the pre-war players would have lost their best years while in the army and some famous names would be heading for the end of their playing careers. The board were worried that Foweraker, as part of the old school, may favour the older players to the detriment of the new ones developing stature in the eyes of the fans. After almost fifty years at the club Foweraker would have to hand over the reins sooner or later, and Walter Rowley was the obvious successor.

Rowley himself was a loyal servant of Bolton Wanderers. He had been signed as a player in 1912 from neighbours Oldham Athletic, and had played 175 games before injury forced him to retire in 1925. During a succession of coaching jobs at Burnden Park Foweraker had been grooming Rowley as a replacement for himself. The title of secretary manager that Foweraker carried was a reflection on the style his management took. The players were used to a system whereby their day-to-day work would be with a chief coach and the decision-making, contracts and team selection would come from the more distant secretary manager. Walter Rowley was preparing to emulate his mentor's methods so that his imminent move would be very much a kick 'upstairs'.

In the desert changes were also about to be made. The duties carried out by the 53rd in Iraq were largely ones of guarding and maintaining the status quo. Major Greenhalgh was getting frustrated at this lack of proper military activity. He was a professional soldier who believed that his unit should be involved in more direct action. It was doubtful that his driver would have concurred. In fact, Ray Westwood was more than a little concerned when the entire Regiment was sent to the Middle East Mountain Warfare Training Centre in the Lebanon.

The journey itself was made in eight stages, following an accustomed route across the desert from Baghdad to Mafraq, thence northwards through Damascus and Homs to Tripoli. There had been no specific orders as to where they were destined after that, only rumours. The terrain in which the Wanderers were now having to operate gave few clues. The first week at the centre had been spent in individual and company training with pack mules. These were to become their main means of transportation for ammunition and supplies when they moved into the Jebel Liban Mountains behind Tripoli for a series of exercises. Over the next few weeks they would be involved in movements by day and night, either in motor transport or more often on foot with the pack transport. Each of these codenamed exercises would last two or three days, followed by a brief rest period before culminating in an all-out four-day assault practise. With limited knowledge of global geography many believed that in view of their attachment to the 8th Indian they were to be sent to fight the Japanese in Asia. A prospect that scared Ray witless.

Back in Brierley Hill the locals had been witnessing a piece of the war unfolding on their own doorsteps. Even in the heart of the Black Country prisoner of war camps had been established to contain the increasing numbers of enemy militia men who had been captured overseas and shipped to England for internment. Over the coming months the Brierley Hill prisoner of war camp was to become dominated by Italians. Each morning the prisoners would be marched from their camp at the bottom of the hill past the Westwood household to their place of work at the top end of the street. In the evening they would be marched back down. The infant Alan Westwood was intrigued. He would watch them, even talk to them. On one occasion a prisoner handed Alan a meticulously carved toy, but most of the adult population of the town who were unused to the sight of foreigners would merely peer inquisitively from behind closed curtains as the Italians marched by.

One evening as the prisoners of war strode into the distance a solitary Royal Navy sailor walked slowly up the road behind them as if looking for something or someone. He paused in front of the Westwood house where Fanny was playing in the garden with Alan.

'Mrs Westwood?' he enquired. Fearing the worst Fanny's heart sank. 'I've got news of your Ray.'

The sailor went on to explain that he had been serving on board the ship which had transported the 53rd Field Regiment to Italy some months earlier. When he had got talking to Ray the sailor realised they were from the same part of the Black Country and he had agreed to look up Ray's family on his next leave, and tell them he had seen Ray safely arriving in Italy. Reassured by the news Fanny thanked the sailor and went into the house to relay the message to Ray's parents. It had always made the waiting at home easier to bear when Fanny had been able to paint a mental picture of where Ray was stationed. Unfortunately with the grim news of heavy casualties in this particular theatre of war she could not dispel the tormented images of her husband in the thick of the action in Italy.

EIGHT

The Italian defence caved in even before an Allied soldier had set foot on the mainland. From the moment a state of emergency was declared in southern Italy on 13 May 1943, in the wake of fears of an Allied invasion, the first grumblings of discontent with Mussolini's fascist party were heard. By mid-June most of the Italian islands in the Mediterranean had fallen to the Allies. A month later the first troops were to step ashore in Sicily as the initial bombing raids were unleashed on Rome. Amid this turmoil Mussolini was spirited away by the Nazis to crisis talks with Hitler in the north of the country. Seizing on this opportunity the anti-fascist Marshal Badoglio fuelled the demonstrations that would lead to the abolition of the Fascist party, and asked the Allies for peace terms. King Victor Emmanuel, who had acquiesced during the fascist regime, finally emerged from the shadows to assume command of the armed forces. The Allies continued to apply pressure to achieve a total submission. The mainland air-raids were extended to target the northern cities of Turin and Milan, even as the coastal assault on Naples began in earnest. Within 24 hours of the Allied capture of Reggio di Calabria, a vital centre on the 'toe' of Italy, the newly appointed prime minister and chief of government, Pietro Badoglio, signed an unconditional surrender. This sudden capitulation caught the Nazis by surprise, in much the same way as the Belgian collapse in 1940 had caught the British napping.

By the time the 53rd Field Regiment of the Bolton Artillery had landed at Taranto, deep inside the 'heel' of Italy, on 24 September 1943, the Allies had established a continuous line of defence across the entire country from the Adriatic to the Tyrrhenian Sea. Three days later Harry Goslin and his unit had penetrated as far north as Foggia, on the eastern side of the Apennines, without meeting any opposition, and were therefore unaware of the stiff resistance the Germans were mounting in Naples on the far side of this mountain range.

Many Italians did not view this as a defeat, or an enemy invasion, but rather as a liberation from Mussolini's tyranny. They welcomed the troops with open arms. Even as they mourned the futile loss of their own sons and fathers they cheered and applauded their liberators. They wanted to display their gratitude in a way the Allies would appreciate. A celebratory football match was to be played at the Foggia stadium, between the home team and what was effectively the 'Wartime Wanderers'.

Jimmy Gittens had been involved in most of the scams that had gone down since the day he was drafted, but on this occasion he was too slow to see a golden opportunity. Another NCO, no doubt with the collusion of Ernie Forrest, drew on his limited knowledge of Hinduism, the predominant religion among the 8th Indian Division to whom they were attached, and negotiated the wholesale exchange of milk rations for beer rations. By the time of the match they had virtually cornered the market. As the spectators poured into the stadium Ernie and his chums cleaned up. The unit's entire beer allotment sold out in an afternoon.

A few days later the Regiment was to follow the Commandos into Termoli and begin the advance on the Adriatic front that was to see the 'Wanderers' embroiled in some of the heaviest, costliest and most prolonged fighting of the Second World War. Ahead of them lay a succession of rivers, each posing a major obstacle that had to be overcome. The Biferno and the Trigno were reached and crossings secured at a high casualty price, especially among the infantry who had spearheaded the attacks. As this intensive action was being launched Italy completed her military about-face and declared war on Germany. Having stripped King Victor Emmanuel of all his titles and thereby abolished the monarchy, Marshal Badoglio urged the Italian soldiers to fight against the Germans 'to their last man,' because of Germany's 'repeated and intensified acts of war'. The retreating Nazi's took revenge on their Italian 'betrayers' and subjected the indigenous population of Naples to a five-day reign of terror. German soldiers roamed the city almost at random, looting and blowing up buildings. Hospitals were attacked to destroy their stocks of food. Water mains and sewers were dynamited to foul water supplies. Thousands of civilians died and many more were crammed into sealed trains and taken under heavy guard to Germany where they were forced into slave labour.

With Naples eventually under the firm control of the Allies Harry Goslin and his men found themselves deployed a little over a mile from their next strategic objective, the River Sangro. As the high level plan of attack was being formulated Montgomery had told his commanders, 'this crossing of the Sangro will be such a crack it will be heard all over Europe'. Before his words could become a prophecy the weather deteriorated, impeding the army's movement and causing the river to reach flood level. The attack was postponed.

The main problem was not so much the actual crossing of the river, but the securing of the strongly defended ridge beyond the open ground on the other side. Jimmy Gittens looked down on this objective from his Bren gun emplacement in a bombed-out building. In accordance with the previously conceived plan the Gurkha unit attached to their division succeeded in crossing the bridge and with the support of an artillery barrage launched their assault on Mozzagrogna, a key point on that ridge. Machine-gun nests and mortar posts dug into the hillside poured merciless fire down the slopes. Undeterred the Gurkhas pushed forward. By the early hours of the morning they were halfway to their objective. Then, after fierce and prolonged hand-to-hand fighting the Gurkhas were forced to withdraw before a ferocious counter-attack by an armoured force using flame-throwers, and artillery. An officer stood in the gaping opening of the building where Jimmy was crouching and pointed to their target, the enemy beyond the river who were at that moment realigning their guns. Jimmy's protestations that they were sitting targets, was met with the officer's retort, 'They'll not be interested in us, they'll be aiming for the OP behind us.' This was hardly a comforting notion as they heard the first salvo of 100-pounders sail overhead with a terrific whistle and rush of air. Four landed within 30 yards of the house before the enemy turned their attention further up the craggy hillside.

Harry Goslin, who was now the subject of this concentrated bombardment, held his ground. A small hut which five officers were using as an observation HQ nearby received a direct hit. Despite being completely buried they all miraculously escaped with only bruises. Donny Howe was less fortunate. As the shelling intensified he was wounded, and under continuous fire was evacuated to a dressing station.

The following night, in what was to be a virtual re-run of the earlier operation, the Allies were successful. With the coming dawn a supporting flank attack saw Mozzagrogna fall and the bridge over the River Sangro placed firmly in Allied hands.

By Wednesday 1 December the northward advance was continuing apace but the Bolton Regiment was still in its same position on the banks of the Sangro as priority on the roads had been given to the tanks. Billy Ainscow was in the temporary motor pool, a small level plateau recessed in the escarpment, with Ray Westwood and Stan Hanson. Suddenly a wave of enemy fighter bombers descended from the low cloud cover and attacked the entire gun area. Recalling their drill Ray, Billy and Stan ran and dived for cover, only to find themselves lying almost vertical against the grass bank bordering the plateau. As the aftershock reverberated in their ears they were conscious of the ensuing machine-gun fire and froze in fear. When the planes receded and calmness returned they were able to assess the casualties: 11 wounded and one fatality – Battery Sergeant Major J. Light, who had won the DCM with the Regiment in 1940.

The advance resumed towards the River Moro. Here in the rugged terrain of the Apennines their training at the Middle East Mountain Warfare Training Centre was truly to come to the fore. In this mountainous region of Italy for the first time in some years Jack Atkinson was to find himself once more in the same theatre of action as his team mates from Bolton, only now he was attached to the Lancashire Fusiliers. Jack had arrived at the Moro camp during a brief respite in the action. Bill Robertson, who had been a regular supporter of the Wanderers before the war, and had even gained some summertime employment at the club painting the players' bar, immediately recognised this former centre-half when he reported for duty, and nabbed him for their own football team. Having mislaid his boots Jack Atkinson took to the pitch for this inter-company match wearing PE shoes, far from ideal footwear in the slippery winter conditions. But for Jack and all other footballers it would be these games played out in every conceivable location, in a multitude of environments, amid violent climatic changes, that they would remember in vivid detail for the rest of their lives. The horrors of the battle action they would shunt to the back of their minds.

Jack had actually managed to see out the 1942/43 season at home, appearing no fewer than ten times in Northern League fixtures, including the very last match on 1 May, before being posted abroad, and relinquishing his position to the young amateur Dan Murphy. Having been spotted in a junior league match Dan was offered a trial with the Wanderers' second team, as a result of which he was to become a regular for the remainder of the war years although he would not be officially signed to play for them until 1945. By the end of the 1942/43 season Nat Lofthouse had added another 25 games and 14 goals to his Bolton tally. He was obviously becoming a regular player and would therefore have been entitled to the increased fee of two pounds per game that the Football Association Management Committee had sanctioned at the beginning of the new season, even though this was being limited to just 14 players at each club. As another fillip to the financially strapped clubs who were also having to contend with the constraints of material rationing, the Board of Trade had agreed to give 40,000 clothing coupons to the professional teams for the purchase of new kit.

As the war dragged on there were other maturing players who were to rise from the second team into the first during the 1943/44 season, such as the former Morecambe Grammar School centre-forward Middlesborough, who had been the junior team's top scorer. But like so many before him this 18-year-old's residency was to be short-lived as he was called into the armed services, a fate that could so easily have befallen Nat Lofthouse now that he had turned conscription age.

At the beginning of December 1943 the British Labour minister Ernest Bevin announced a ballot scheme the government was introducing to combat the severe manpower shortage. One out of every ten 18 to 25-year-olds conscripted would be ordered to work down the mines. If there were any critics who thought when Nat turned up for his first shift at the Mossley Colliery that his was a soft option, they should have taken heed of the example set by many young miners who were volunteering for the forces just so they could escape the rigours of the pits.

As Nat's thoughts were preoccupied with the daunting prospect of descending into the unknown depths of an alien mine shaft Harry Goslin and his men were ascending the mountains west of Treglio. The crossing of the River Moro had been accomplished by a Canadian division on the night of 9/10 December, with the aid of a deception plan fired by the Bolton Artillery and others in the 8th Indian. Four days later they were still dug into the mountainside several thousand feet above sea level. Jack Atkinson was employed as a driver of 15 hundredweight trucks ferrying equipment and ammunition to Bill Robertson's Lancashire Fusiliers who were entrenched on the lower slopes. From there the matériel was relayed via pack mule to the artillery. The difficult terrain and the torrential winter rains that began to lash the region temporarily halted the Allied advance enabling the Germans to hold and reinforce a defensive line from Pescara on the Adriatic to Minturno on the Mediterranean, where their main western

force was incarcerated in the virtually impregnable fortress of the
Monte Cassino monastery several miles inland.

With reinforcements pouring south to strengthen their rearguard the
Germans launched a major counter offensive. On 14 December the
shelling of Goslin's OP area intensified. He had taken over the position
that morning and had no time to relocate the post from the slit trench
that had been dug dangerously close to the tree line. As the shell bursts
assailed his senses Harry's OP signaller, Gunner Plummer, was killed
by a sniper's bullet. Harry had no time to react before another round
exploded in the tree directly above him, viciously perforating his back
with splinters and shrapnel. Bill Robertson was well aware of the
pounding these men were taking higher up the mountain, but was still
taken aback when a panic-stricken soldier came running from the trees
shouting, 'Anyone here from Bolton? Wanderers' captain's been
killed.' Jimmy Gittens was in the command post when Ernie Forrest
burst in with the stretcher-bearers carrying Harry Goslin, still alive but
bleeding profusely, and barely conscious. For the first time Ernie was
speechless. Tears welled in his eyes. Harry was invincible. Because of
him the entire Bolton Wanderers team was invincible. The Germans
had struck their Achilles' heel. Harry died a few days later, only weeks
after his 35th birthday.

This was a major tragedy that mysteriously went unrecorded in the
Bolton Evening News of 18 December. Perhaps they did not wish to
damage morale, or more likely the news had not yet reached them.
Although the front page carried a report from a Reuters special
correspondent applauding the Allies' success in repelling the counter-
offensive that claimed Harry's life, their sports writer, 'The Tramp',
was more concerned with the ongoing problems at Burnden Park. As
the team turned out at Maine Road to play Manchester United in their
last game before Christmas they were subjected to the now familiar
shake-up, with no fewer than six positional changes to the side.
Lofthouse began the game well before a crowd of 5,000, but despite
showing cleverness in the attack, and a superb early low diving header
that had the United goalkeeper stretched full length, a tactic that was
to win Nat the epithet 'torpedo', the defence could not contain the
situation as the Manchester forwards repeatedly pressed into the
Bolton penalty area. By half-time Manchester were a goal ahead. An
equaliser from Gorman momentarily stemmed the advance, but did
nothing to reverse it. United's 3–1 victory was destined to be repeated
in the return leg at Burnden Park on Christmas Day, after the host
team had undergone yet another five changes in their line-up.

For the survivors of Harry Goslin's unit Christmas was just another day of heavy fighting for the control of the Ortona-Orsogna-Guariagrele lateral road that was facing off the enemy's armoured front, which they had named the Gustav Line. For the Bolton players the battle was raging in a country where knife-edged rocks slashed boots and leggings to ribbons. In the western sector the Americans were advancing laboriously in knee-deep mud along the valley of the Gariglione (the 'Gargling River'), the two armies unavoidably bent on merging for a confrontation at Monte Cassino.

On 1 January 1944 King Victor Emmanuel made another bid to ingratiate himself with his people in a radio speech broadcast from the relatively safe Adriatic port of Brindisi:

> There is but one duty and one right for all – to serve our country loyally, to liberate her as soon as possible from the foe who tortures and oppresses her.
>
> Let every personal resentment be overcome, every special project postponed. Let us give our all for our country that it may soon and surely rise again in full liberty.
>
> As the New Year begins your King wishes to be near you and asks nothing more than to be the first to serve Italy.

By that New Year's Day the 53rd's situation had changed to a holding position as both sides maintained their own ground separated by only a marginal no-man's-land. As a mark of respect for the late Harry Goslin the teams at Burnden Park lined up before the centre stand and stood for a moment's silence, every one of the Bolton Wanderers players wearing a sombre black armlet. The day before, football writer 'The Tramp' had published the first and only obituary to their hero: 'Harry Goslin was one of the finest types professional football breeds. Not only in a personal sense, but for the club's sake, and the game's sake. I regret his life has had to be sacrificed in the cause of war.'

The Bolton Regiment was to remain in action in the most appalling winter conditions right up to early April, when they were eventually relieved by the 31st Field Regiment and moved back to the safety of Guglionesi, a lush haven on the banks of the Biferno, the first river they had conquered all those months before. Stan Hanson, however, had found himself at this rest camp a month earlier. While Nat Lofthouse was contributing two goals to the home team's 6–1 defeat of Bury at Burnden Park on 4 March Stan was making a similar impact on the 8th Army's 6–2 victory over the Yugoslav Partisans, in his debut performance as a left-winger. It was one of those rare opportunities that presented themselves in the midst of the hostilities. Stan was not officially on leave and had only found himself briefly out of the action as a transit driver between the front line and the rest camp. The position of goalkeeper had already gone to Swinnerton, another professional, when Stan was brought into the side. A crowd of five thousand turned out to see the match that was reported two days later in the *Eighth Army News*, a publication provided by the Psychological Warfare Branch. Their reporter at the game commented: 'Hanson's speed seems to be wasted between the posts. He made many dazzling runs down the wing, and only once did I see him out of position for a pass from Rudd.' Stan Hanson also managed to secure two goals, the first being made for him by Jackson, the six times Scottish international, and the second was a magnificent header that even Lofthouse would have been proud of.

But for the rest of the Regiment when they arrived in Guglionesi there was to be little time for reflection, and no serious football, only knockabouts. Their days were absorbed in special boat training, and the overhaul, modification and calibration of the guns. On 15 April 1944 they received information that the Regiment would be moving into action on the 27th, south of Cassino. Recce and digging parties, including Ernie Forrest and Ray Westwood as drivers, left the very next morning.

In those last weeks of the football season Nat had to face the reality that the war had finally come to Bolton. As he left for his early shift at the colliery he passed rows of armoured vehicles, lorries and jeeps lining the back streets. Throughout spring Britain had become one huge armed camp as the Allies prepared for their invasion of fortress Europe. All coastal areas were banned to visitors. Overseas travel by foreign diplomats stationed in London was forbidden. Throughout the country fake concentrations of troops and dummy ships were deployed to keep the enemy guessing as to when and where the Allied assault would be mounted. Railway timetables were completely rescheduled to enable the swift mobilisation of hundreds of thousands of British, American and Commonwealth troops to the various invasion assembly points.

Nat was hardening through his life as a miner. It was not uncommon for him to start his six-hour shift well before dawn, then surface at midday to catch a tram to the ground in order to play a full ninety minutes of professional football against opponents several years his senior. His romance with Alma was also going from strength to strength, not least because of the genuine compassion he had displayed when she received word that her soldier friend had been killed in action. While this entire character-building experience certainly contributed to his growing success both on and off the pitch there were still times when Nat felt he should be standing shoulder to shoulder with his heroes, that hard core of players like Ray Westwood and Ernie Forrest who had been fighting in foreign lands for going on two years.

They were now encamped at Monte Cairo, five miles north-west of Cassino, situated on Highway Number 6, the main road from Naples to Rome. The heavily fortified Monastery Hill was about one mile due west of the town. The River Rapido entered Cassino from the north, and left it flowing south as the Gari to its confluence with the Liri. An area bounded by these rivers and the road running south from Cassino through San Angelo was known as the Liri Appendix. It was from here that the Allied general offensive was to be launched. As early as February 142 Flying Fortresses and 87 medium bombers had dropped 450 tons of bombs on the Monte Cassino Abbey alone, in preparation for the first Allied offensive undertaken by the 2nd New Zealand Corps. After attack and counter attack they were forced to withdraw. A month later carpet bombing of the town by 500 planes still failed to eliminate the opposition. By early May the German defensive position remained intact. To achieve this deadlock it had already cost the New Zealanders 4,000 casualties.

For Ray, Ernie, Stan and the others it must have seemed a daunting prospect. No matter the battles they had won, with minimum loss of their inner circle, to face Cassino without Harry was to be their 'charge of the light brigade'. Ernie was philosophical, still trying to find humour in the tightest situation. Stan was unmoved. Nothing ever seemed to worry him. Or if it did, he refused to show it. He had risen to the rank of Lance Corporal, and that was good enough. Of the Wanderers only Ray had failed to win any stripes, and that also suited him fine.

With one OP sited on Mount Trocchio to their rear the Commanding Officer was in a unique position to control the fire of all four field regiments under his command. Their objective was to establish a bridgehead which would then enable them to clear the entire Liri Appendix. As the offensive was about to start the Allied Commander-in-Chief, General Alexander, told his men, 'Throughout the past winter you have fought hard and valiantly . . . tomorrow we can see victory ahead. We are going to destroy the German armies in Italy.'

At 2300 hours on the night of 11 May 1944 the great artillery programme commenced. The expected heavy mist that invariably preceded dawn was now thickened by a dense fog caused by the gun smoke fired from both sides, with the result that visibility along the front lines was reduced to just one yard. The torrent whirling at the confluence of the Liri and the Gari added to the confusion by creating such a swift current that many assault boats were completely washed away. Against these odds a limited bridgehead had been forged under intense enemy shelling and mortaring. When the sun finally broke through the cordite and mist cloud at about 1030 the infantry unit the Bolton Artillery were supporting found their slit trenches in full view of a nearby crossroads registered by the Germans. Abandoning their wireless equipment they had to make a dash for cover. As fast as these lines of communication were severed the maintenance teams renewed the links with the OPs and the gunners. Throughout the day the battle increased in ferocity. Still the Allies managed to consolidate their all too narrow bridgehead.

Another artillery bombardment 24 hours after the first, supported by tanks, managed to gain some ground but by mid-afternoon on the 13th was met by an enemy counter attack, which was effectively broken up by the fire of the field regiments, a significant achievement that bred the feeling that the enemy resistance was decreasing. By the following day they had successfully cleared the Liri Appendix and established a firm base from where to launch their final assault on the still heavily fortified Monastery Hill. An assault that was to last another nine days.

Midway through the battle, with the hill now isolated and under concentrated attack, the Bolton Regiment were ordered to move back to Dragoni for a few days' rest. In an air of false security the 'Wanderers' took to a makeshift pitch to unwind and block out the strain and horror of the battlefront.

At home the boards were once again going up at Burnden Park for the close season, Bolton having lost their last match to Liverpool on Saturday 13 May. This defeat placed them 48th in the Football League Northern Section, in what was to be their worst result of the war years. It was now Nat's turn to unwind; he had scored Bolton's last goal of the season pushing his total to 15 and placing him second highest for the year. But he could take some solace in the knowledge that he had played nine fewer games than the top scorer, Currie, who had just 17 to his credit. Nat's continually improving physique and stamina, not to mention his bulldog determination, he would later attribute to his labours down the mine, an assertion that would have to wait until the autumn to be put to the test. For now he would relax at the Empress with Alma. Her close friend Eileen was away in London, working as a teleprint operator in the Whitehall dungeons of the War Office, but there were many other former pupils of Castle Hill who were now regulars at the dance hall, including Joyce Hazelton, who unbeknown to her was destined to marry a Trotter she had yet to meet, Ernie Forrest.

Ernie must have thought somebody upstairs had it in for the Bolton Wanderers when they were ordered back into action south-west of Cassino. The entire area was already a devastated wasteland when the 53rd commenced yet another concentrated barrage on the morning of 23 May. By nightfall there was the growing impression that the enemy had ordered a general withdrawal. As if that seemingly constant exchange of high-calibre fire for weeks on end had not been frightening enough they were now being asked to wage a fierce house-to-house battle among the crumbled ruins of buildings to rout out snipers, machine-gunners and the few anti-tank guns still remaining. Billy Ainscow recalls running from the shattered shell of a house and glancing back to see who was following him only to catch sight of a fellow artilleryman receiving a direct shell burst as he was framed in the doorway. A blinding flash, a cordite cloud and the soldier was obliterated.

Two days later the Allied armies were shaking hands in Monte Cassino. The spine of the German defence had been broken. What remained of the enemy was on the run. As the 53rd advanced towards Rome in close support of the 19th Brigade they met little opposition. A nominal effort by the rearguard of a retreating German parachute division was soon dealt with. Even the more stubborn resistance at the Lucinetta feature in the Simbruini Mountains near Guarcino was rapidly put down with no Allied casualties.

This action coincided with the Regiment receiving the first news that the Americans were in Rome. The following day King Victor Emmanuel officially abdicated in favour of Crown Prince Umberto. As the D-Day landings were being effected on the Normandy coast the Italians celebrated the freedom of their eternal city, and the return to democracy under the provisional leadership of the ex-premier Ivanoe Bonomi. The 53rd were still in the Apennines east of Rome awaiting outlines of the divisional plan that would see them continuing the Allied northward advance.

By the middle of June the Bolton Artillery's operation had become a matter of fire and movement, such as they had practised so keenly at Larkhill prior to their posting to the Middle East. Their progress was now rapid. Each day they were to be bivouacked in a new location, as if on a package tour, but it was no holiday when they suffered brief outbursts of German resistance as at Foligno, which resulted in the Allies' swift capture of some 100 prisoners and a large number of horses. Although stiffer opposition was mounted at Bastia on entering neighbouring Assisi, the OPs found the town miraculously clear and unspoiled, as if sheltering under the protection of their patron saint, Francis. The Regiment was now deep inside the province of Umbria and by the end of the month was encamped at Perugia, the enemy forced back into a defensive position at Florence with their front, the 'Gothic Line', being established at the River Arno.

The Bolton artillerymen came out of action on 30 June, and the next day found themselves on a whirlwind sight-seeing tour of the capital, a respite from the action that was welcomed and appreciated by most. Ray, however, chose to spend his recreational leave with Ernie and Stan at the American army base, where he could indulge his passion for chocolate. They also accepted a challenge on behalf of their team-mates to face the Americans on the football pitch. Believing this would be a soft touch Ernie and Ray wasted no time in soliciting Jimmy Gittens's help in running a book. One can only imagine their surprise when they lined up to face what was obviously a squad of 'South' Americans. Undeterred, they kicked off, and Ray was in top form, swerving through the front line and bursting past his midfield marker, but every single time his way would be blocked by a burly six-foot-plus black defender. They had come up against a team that were playing with a 'sweeper', a style of football not taken up in Europe until the 1970s.

The Wartime Wanderers had been in action almost continuously since their arrival in Italy, and only now did they get paid. But not in time to go on a spending spree in the capital. Instead, the paymaster dolled out their ten months' back pay as they were being returned to the front. It was still a few months until Stan's wedding anniversary but not knowing when he would next get leave he handed £25 over to an officer who was being posted to Naples, with the request to get something nice for 'Maisie'.

As they headed back into action it was clear that the war was taking its toll. Ray had suffered repeated attacks of dysentery and other more exotic diseases since his first infection in Egypt, but they had failed to secure him a ticket home. There was some suggestion that there was an element of malingering, which Ray would neither admit nor refute. Certainly his continued position as the CO's driver had kept him out of the heaviest action, and he could barely recall the few occasions he actually performed the duty of his title, 'Gunner' Westwood. Ernie, on the other hand, had been in the thick of it too much, and like Jack Hurst and many of the others he was beginning to go deaf. So it was with even greater relief that instead of returning to the front line part of their unit was sent south to the coastal town of Salerno for six clear days' leave. Stan Hanson's detachment would be sent once Ray and the others returned.

As Ernie descended the winding track from the mountain-top front-line HQ to the foothills of the Apennines en route for leave he had glanced in the rear view mirror and seen what he believed to be a speeding vehicle wishing to pass. Pulling over to the gravel verge he was amazed to see his own gun trailer, complete with its 25-pounder, go sailing past on a terminal collision course with the rock face. Ernie was probably not surprised therefore when a detailed equipment inspection at the Eighth Army Rest Camp was to condemn eleven guns and twenty-three Quads in their regiment alone, a clear indication of the punishment both men and machinery were taking in the Italian campaign.

What they had anticipated as a recreational leave was fast becoming a busman's holiday. The signals officer ran a class for driver operators, which both Ernie and Ray were expected to attend, in addition to which all gunners had to undergo an instruction course on the new 75mm gun and other replacement equipment being run by one of the battery captains and a small support team. So it would not be until they were heading back into action that they would be allowed to indulge their other skills.

Arriving in Foligno, to enable the remainder of their detachment to retire to Salerno for a well deserved rest, the army commandeered the local football stadium to stage the inter-regimental match between the 52nd Field Regiment and the Bolton Wanderers' 53rd. No matter the teams were still battle-weary, this was sport and for Ray, Ernie, Stan and the bulk of their side, it was also their profession which ensured their five goals to one victory.

It was a hollow success. No sooner had the final whistle blown than Stan learnt that the leave planned for the remainder of the unit was to be cancelled as the entire brigade's period of rest was abruptly terminated with the receipt of dispatches that saw them deployed to relieve the Central European Force, who in turn had received orders to seize the crossing over the River Arno west of Florence. The Regiment quickly got into its stride advancing rapidly with the support of tanks and mortars into Siena, through Montepello and on to the French-occupied Castelfiorentino. The main obstruction to their progress now was Ernie's worst nightmare: mines. Already the 53rd's Q Battery had lost one killed and five wounded on their approach to this hillside retreat. With the Royal Engineers busy elsewhere the gunners and their crews had to sweep their own immediate areas as best they could. In the midst of this operation Q Battery was to suffer another great loss when the jeep carrying their commander, Major Hart, went up on a mine. Together with the less seriously injured driver and signaller he was evacuated to the field hospital near Siena where he died shortly after admission.

Although there were still a few pockets of enemy south of the Arno the infantry advance was so swift that the artillery was often out of range before they were able to redeploy. As the Germans withdrew from Florence to the 'Gothic Line', a fortified position they had constructed along the forward crest of the northern Apennines, the 53rd and other regiments engaged in a continuous series of reliefs along the banks of the river to either side of the city as part of a deception plan prior to launching a major assault on the German lines. Once again Ray Westwood was lucky to avoid this tit-for-tat exercise as he drove their CO, Lieutenant Colonel Greenhalgh, to Rome for a conference with the Commander of the Eighth Army who was to impart top-secret information on Allied plans for the immediate future. On 25 August 1944, with the 53rd now encamped on the plains of Lombardy, a personal message was read to all ranks giving a general outline of the plan to break through the 'Gothic Line', with the aid of a vast army that had been secretly assembled on the far side of the mountains in the Adriatic Sector.

As the Bolton Artillery ascended the Apennines to embark on yet another long and bloody battle in extremely difficult terrain, hampered by intense cold, rain and snow, the new football season got off to an unimaginative start with a goalless draw for Bolton at home to Halifax before a crowd of 6,500. Nat Lofthouse was to miss this opening match, and another nine games in the first half of the year, so the club was not to feel the real benefit of his vastly improved abilities until the later stages of the competition. A performance that was ironically to have its parallel on the battlefield.

Progress was slow in country that afforded good observation to the enemy and both leading battalions were soon to suffer enormous casualties from the heavy German shelling. Under this continuous fire directed by the enemy OPs on the higher ground ahead the Bolton Artillery laboriously advanced by batteries up the slopes of Abetina. A surprise counter-attack on the night of 2/3 September saw an Argyll company commander and his two platoons virtually surrounded by the enemy. The 53rd dug in and prepared a fire plan to support their attempted withdrawal to a less exposed position. Two minutes before the bombardment was to commence a heavy thunderstorm broke and thick cloud obscured the moon. Torrential rain and dense mist now combined to handicap the infantry who even had difficulty in maintaining direction. With the coming dawn the troops were still pinned down by machine-gun and mortar fire from three sides. Only a successful smoke screen laid down by Q Battery of the Bolton Artillery enabled them to escape. It was evidently clear that the enemy were holding the mountain ridges so strongly that only an attack at full army level would now have any chance of a breakthrough.

Orders for the attack were received by the 53rd on 7 September, but postponed, and then cancelled when it became apparent that the enemy had relinquished its advantage and pulled out, a tactic that was to be repeated time and again over the coming weeks and months. Always maintaining the higher ground they would retreat from range to range with the Allies in relentless pursuit. Land so gained by the Eighth Army was often lost to a ferocious German counter-attack fought in the worst possible geographic and climatic conditions. At times the troops found themselves wading through mud two feet deep. Bulldozers became bogged down. Often the only way to mount the guns on their platforms was with the use of four oxen. With supply lines similarly affected ammunition expenditure was initially limited to 100 rounds per day for each battalion in the line. The ensuing mountain storms which flooded the creeks and rivers all but brought the offensive to a standstill. Only when a slight improvement in the weather attracted a resurgence of enemy fire did they increase this allotment to 120 rounds.

Elsewhere in the European theatre the Allies had launched a day and night assault on Dunkirk. Fighters and fighter bombers had attacked German troop concentrations, artillery and transportation targets in support of the Allied ground forces in Holland. Active aerial patrolling was being maintained along the German border from Aachen to Luxembourg. In the area north-east of Nancy, close to the France-Belgium frontier, Allied soldiers had advanced into the Forêt de

Gremecey and installed themselves on the high ground overlooking the occupied towns of Fresnes en Saunois and Coutures.

Nat Lofthouse had by that time opened his account, netting his first two goals of the season in the 5–0 victory against Oldham at Burnden Park. He also had other reasons to be jubilant. Both the Football League and the Association were about to hold their annual meeting that among other things was to discuss the future of professional football after the war and Everton's proposal that the players' wages should be increased from eight to nine pounds. There was even speculation that they would lobby the government for legislation that would see proceeds from the football pools allocated to improving stadiums and providing gymnasia for training. Following hard on this news was Mr Bevin's announcement that those, like Nat, who had been working down the mines would be treated as if they had been in the army, and would be released from their compulsory employment down the pits as soon as practical after the cessation of hostilities.

It was almost prophetic that as Nat's own situation stabilised and his now permanent presence contributed to the changing fortunes of the Trotters, so did the circumstances of the 53rd Field Regiment begin to improve. After three and a half months of continuous fighting just one battery was to be granted permission for a ten-day leave at a rest area near Florence. Stan Hanson was one of the lucky ones to be pulled out of action. It was almost Christmas when Stan learnt that May had received his gift of an expensive silk bed quilt on 26 September, their wedding anniversary. While on leave Stan was asked to take a seriously shellshocked soldier out on the town, and show him a good time, a task the army could obviously trust Stan to do responsibly. But even the heavy drinking session that ensued did nothing to make the soldier forget the horrors he had endured. His injuries obviously went far deeper than the army doctors realised, for the unknown soldier died the day after.

General Sir Harold Alexander, Allied Commander in Italy, had been able to confirm in a press conference that during the previous six months half of Germany's original forces in Italy, equivalent to fifteen full-strength divisions, had been wiped out. The Tactical Air Forces supporting the advance had flown over 132,000 sorties, dropped 69,000 tons of bombs and destroyed 311 enemy planes. Sappers had cleared 16,800 mines and the German war matériel captured had included 340 tanks, 260 assault guns, 540 anti-tank guns, 204 other artillery pieces and 339 locomotives. In the wake of the Allied armies the engineers had repaired 9,300 miles of roads, including 21 miles of bridging, and rebuilt more than 1,000 miles of Italian railway over which 25,000 war trains were carrying troops and supplies. Five major seaports had been reconstructed and had handled over 180,000 men and more than one million tons of supplies between them.

It was hardly surprising, therefore, that in the light of this statement that had been published so soon after the news that the German army in Greece was on the point of capitulation and the recently published reports that the Home Guard were to be stood down, that many people in England believed that victory was now in sight. In his characteristic style the Prime Minister, Winston Churchill, warned the House of Commons and the country against any indulgence in the feeling that the war would soon be over: 'It may be, but do not indulge that feeling,' he declared. 'The truth is that no one knows when the German war will be finished, and still less how long the interval will be between the defeat of the Germans and the defeat of the Japanese.' Recalling his previous forecast that the war with Germany would last until the early summer of 1945, Churchill added, 'My personal inclination is not at all to mitigate this forecast. Indeed, if I were to make any change in the unfolding of events it would be to leave out the word "early" before the word "summer".'

It was Walter Rowley's painful duty to notify the board of directors and the players that Charles Foweraker's protégé, Walter Sidebottom, had been killed when his ship was torpedoed in the English Channel.

The original 'Gothic Line' had been long surrendered when the Bolton Artillery laid down another fire plan on an area beyond the River Senio in the week before Christmas. But by now the winter conditions were so harsh that little progress could be made. Although the German divisions in Italy actually outnumbered those of the Allies they lacked both armour and air power. What forces they did have their commander, Kesselring, now concentrated on holding their new line through Bologna. Intelligence reports of an intended counter attack against the Allied 8th Army dug in just nine miles from the city meant that the entire Bolton Artillery received orders for a potential mobilisation on 25 December. Not wishing to deny his men their seasonal repast Lieutenant Colonel Greenhalgh decreed that the Regiment would celebrate Christmas on the 24th.

In the event two of the battery commanders were sent to the UK to attend a Long Gunnery Staff Course and Greenhalgh himself was ordered to report to Lucca by the evening of 26 December to act as Artillery Adviser to the Divisional Commander. His long-serving driver, Ray Westwood, believed he was now out of the fire fight for good as they motored leisurely through the unspoilt Tuscan countryside. This valley of the River Serchio is wild and romantic, running through the picturesque district of Garfagnana between the Apuan Mountains and the main chain of the Etruscan Apennines before debouching into the basin of the Arno at the medieval walled town of Lucca. It was felt impractical to attempt a crossing of the mountains at this point and the Allied command therefore treated the sector as a quiet one whose defence was left to a specially enlisted American formation that fell some way short of the very high standard set by the other US divisions.

Even before Greenhalgh and Westwood arrived at their new posting reports began to arrive that the enemy were planning an attack down this valley passing through Lucca to pose a very real threat to the coastal port of Leghorn (Livorno), through which all of the 5th Army's supplies came. The expected assault had actually commenced on Christmas Day, and meeting scant resistance had some initial success in capturing the town of Barga and two small villages. As the American unit withdrew in the wake of this attack they passed through the 8th Indian Division, to whom the Bolton Artillery was attached, now advancing to assume the offensive, strongly supported by the Tactical Air Command. The first of the 53rd's batteries moved into action immediately and within a matter of days they had routed the enemy and restored the status quo. By the first week of January as the remainder of the 53rd took up positions the Serchio Valley had completely reverted to its normal quiet state. No longer required, the entire Bolton Artillery was moved to a rest area at Agnano near Pisa. Only Jack Roberts did not accompany them. In what had probably been their briefest of battles he had been caught in the blast of an enemy shell and had taken heavy shrapnel in the face, detaching the retina, and was immediately invalided out. As his team-mates could only look forward to a tenuous leave in an army camp Jack was shipped home to England, and a long road to recovery.

For those remaining it was to be another all too short rest period, interspersed with only the occasional friendly match. For within a month information arrived from the Headquarters Royal Artillery that the Regiment was once more being ordered to take up a front-line position, in this instance replacing a Canadian field regiment. The existing camouflage was left untouched; even the gun emplacements were to remain unchanged. Following closely behind the recce party that had left the Monte Giorgio area due north of Florence on 24 February the 53rd soon found themselves in action to the west of the

Ravenna-Alfonsine railway. Over the coming weeks the batteries would alternate between the forward firing and primary positions from where they would respond only to direct requests for covering fire.

As Q Battery was being replaced by P Battery on the front line Ernie Forrest, Stan Hanson and what remained of the Trotters found themselves reunited with Ray Westwood as the Regimental football team. They had been in heavy and sustained action for eighteen months solid, with only a few days' leave to recuperate, little enough time to relieve the tension of constant battle, let alone partake in any meaningful training. The perpetual sound of exploding ordnance filled their heads. Images of fallen comrades floated through their memories alongside fading visions of those they had left at home. For Ray, and many like him, they could only create approximate likenesses of the sons and daughters they had never seen. The smell of cordite and fear would linger in their nostrils. But for ninety minutes they would endeavour to push all this to one side and launch into the game with gusto. On this occasion, however, their will was not enough to avert a two goals to three defeat to an RAF Squadron team, which saw the 53rd knocked out of the Fifth Army cup competition, a disappointment to everyone.

At Burnden Park the crowds were gradually creeping back to their pre-war levels, partly due to the receding threat of enemy air-raids and the news from abroad that inclined the public to believe that total victory was now imminent, and partly attributed to the presence of Nat Lofthouse. The combination of his grit and determination and impressive goalscoring record was helping to put the Trotters back on top. Charles Foweraker witnessed this ascension from his regular seat in the directors box. He was not a well man, and had not been for some time, so he had been succeeded in the position of secretary-manager by Walter Rowley. As a mark of respect he had been given a life season ticket, and his own seat. He recalled his first meeting with Nat Lofthouse, and had watched him mature. Now Charles realised with pride that his judgement had been right. Nat's presence alone was beginning to have that magical pulling power associated with star players. Nat had truly arrived, and Alma was proud to be there in the VIP stand cheering on her man.

The Allies were already in Germany when the Bolton Artillery began a month-long campaign to oust the enemy irrevocably from Italy. Three distinct armies were involved pushing north along the shores of both the Adriatic and the Mediterranean while also protecting the flanks of the centre force. Following a wave of heavy bombers that laid down a carpet of fragmentation bombs behind the River Senio there commenced a concentration of artillery fire greater than that put down at Alamein. Ahead lay a succession of rivers to be breached. Defences along the banks of the Santerno, the Reno, and the Po were swiftly forced out of their positions. By the middle of April the capture of Bologna coincided with the Allied occupation of Nuremberg, the scene of huge Nazi rallies in the late 1930s. Exploitation was now rapid. The 8th Army, to which the 53rd was attached, swung north-east towards Padua and Venice. The 5th Army zeroed in on Milan to the north-west, while the American 92nd Division moved along the coast to Genoa and Monaco. Indeed the advance was so swift that Ernie Forrest and his team-mates were to find themselves locked in a traffic jam at the crossing of the River Po.

Billy Ainscow was summoned into the Regimental office to be informed that he was now on holiday. Having served four years without any home leave he was entitled to a month's vacation and they would be flying him out imminently. Billy could not believe it, or understand why he had been singled out. The entire unit qualified under these terms, and therefore he could only assume that the leave was to be rostered on an alphabetical basis. If that was the case then poor old Ray Westwood would have a hell of a wait.

In Milan Italian partisans captured and assassinated Mussolini and his mistress Clara Petacci. Along with an aide their bodies were strung up by their heels from the façade of a petrol station in the Piazza Loretto.

The defenders of the Allies' final obstacle, the Adige, gave up without a fight. In the early hours of 29 April the Bolton Artillery received orders to move forward to Padua and Venice. At 0700 hours Ernie, Stan and Ray leapt behind their steering wheels eager to be off. For the first time in six years even Ray was excited. He could see the end. But an hour later they still had not moved. The road to Padua was choked with their own advancing troops.

By midday Padua had fallen, and by the evening Venice was also in the hands of the Allied 8th Army. The war in Italy was over. The very next day Adolf Hitler shot himself, just hours before the victorious troops descended on his bunker beneath the Berlin Reichstag. Simultaneously Brigadier T.S. Dobree DSO, MC, Commander of the 19th Indian Infantry Brigade, paid an informal visit to the Bolton Artillery now encamped at Sabbioni. Following lunch he visited each of the batteries, and talked to the men, Ernie, Stan, Ray, Jack Hurst,

Jack Roberts, Jimmy Gittens and many others. He thanked them for their hard work, and in particular he congratulated them all on the speed and accuracy of their shooting.

As the *Bolton Evening News* carried a front-page banner headline predicting that the end of the war was now only a matter of hours away the news of the latest German surrender in Holland reached the Gestapo Chief Johl in Denmark, who reportedly went white, sat down trembling and began to weep. The territory he occupied was now also relinquished. Scenes of wild jubilation, in which some of the German soldiers actually joined in, began immediately the release from the Nazi occupation was announced. People lit rolled newspapers for torches, flew the flags of the Allies, danced and embraced in the streets. British soldiers sang in their camps and billets. Everywhere it was felt that this event was only the prelude to the greater capitulation that would be underlined in the last clause of the instrument of surrender.

At 2.41 a.m. on Monday 7 May 1945 peace came to a battered Europe in a small red schoolhouse in Rheims where General Eisenhower, the Allied Supreme Commander, witnessed General Alfred Jodl, the German Army Chief of Staff, sign the instrument of unconditional surrender. Suddenly it was all over, and Britain took to the streets to celebrate the victory.

Back home at Burnden Park Nat was joining in the Wanderers' own celebrations. Before crowds of 30,000 as Bolton's top goal scorer, with a clear majority, Nat had helped secure a place in the Football League War Cup (Northern) Final against those arch rivals, Manchester United. The tournament was to be decided in two legs. These would be the first football matches to be played in the new peaceful era.

NINE

Billy Ainscow had just purchased his first fish and chips in Bolton when he was caught up in the victory celebrations and found himself dancing all the way down Ainsworth Lane. As had been expected Winston Churchill had broadcast the news of the cessation of hostilities simultaneously to London, Washington and Moscow from the Cabinet Room at Number 10 Downing Street. The celebratory atmosphere was as discernible in Whitehall as everywhere else, only heightened by the sight of huge loudspeakers jutting from the corners of the Ministry of Health building. In Germany their new Foreign Minister, Schwerin Krosigk, declared to the German people via the Flensburg Radio, 'After almost six years of struggle we have succumbed. No one must deceive himself as to the severity of the surrender conditions. We had to accept them.'

Europe was now at peace, but the Wartime Wanderers found themselves in limbo, wondering what the future held for them. At this time they did not presume that their fighting days were over. The war in the Far East was still raging intensely. To heighten their fears, they were now ordered to complete additional training that would prepare them for the jungle warfare they would be facing when shipped to that last theatre of action. The army needed to keep the troops busy, but they also needed to bolster morale. There were still football opportunities, especially in the south where the 53rd was based, and the military realised that these matches could keep several thousand men entertained for a whole afternoon. Several of the games were to have an international flavour with the Italians proving to be willing participants in them. One such match was organised against an Italian representative side made up of professionals, including the goalkeeper Gigi Peronace, who could match the Wartime Wanderers' football stature. After the match, which took place in Foggia, the setting for the

Wanderers' very first game in Italy in 1943, Ray Westwood struck up a rapport with the future Italian international, and a friendship was begun that was to last until Peronace's death in the 1970s.

Bolton Wanderers' fortunes had also taken a turn for the better during the 1944/45 season. More players had emerged to become regular first teamers. Malcolm Barrass had made his debut on the opening day of the season, having been signed from the Manchester works team, Ford Motors. Lol Hamlett rose from the reserves to become a regular centre-half and Tommy Woodward, who had been stationed back in England immediately after the Allied victory in North Africa, was an almost permanent fixture on the right wing. For the first time since the beginning of the war Walter Rowley had been able to reduce the numbers of guest players the club needed to call on. In fact only six were to be used throughout the whole of that season. This increased stability and the continuing goalscoring exploits of Nat Lofthouse served to improve the club's League position greatly. In the first half of the season, calculated up until Christmas, Bolton had finished in ninth position, but had slipped back to 15th out of 54 by the time the season finished in May 1945, an auspicious date. But it was Cup glory that had captured the imagination of the Bolton supporters and brought them flocking to the ground. The last eight League games of the season, against Accrington Stanley, Blackpool, Newcastle United and Wolverhampton Wanderers, also counted as ties for the Football League War Cup (North), calculated on a goal aggregate of the home and away fixtures.

After a goalless draw at home to Accrington, Bolton marched through to the next round with a 4–1 win in the away leg in which Nat Lofthouse scored twice. In the next round Bolton had to face Blackpool, the current champions of the Football League North, who had reached the final of the Cup the previous year only to be denied the League and Cup double by losing to Aston Villa. Bolton Wanderers won the away leg 4–1 in front of a Bloomfield Road crowd of 20,000. The match was a personal triumph for Nat who scored all four of Bolton's goals. This was enough to take them through to the next round, despite dropping the home leg 2–1. By then the word had got around town that Bolton Wanderers had a chance in the Cup and a massive 26,000 turned out at Burnden Park for the visit of Newcastle United. This record crowd was to witness a spectacular 3–0 victory by the home side, with Nat Lofthouse notching up another two goals to his Cup tally. The other goal by Malcolm Barrass meant that once again the Wanderers had done enough to carry them into the semi-final regardless of their 4–2 defeat at St James's Park.

Only Wolves now stood in the way of Bolton Wanderers and a place in the final of the Football League War Cup. This time the away leg was played first and Bolton came back from Wolverhampton with a useful 2–2 draw. Everything now hinged on the home leg. In the run up to this meeting the manager of Wolverhampton Wanderers, Ted Vizard, who had been a star player with Bolton way back in the 1920s, was invited to publish his views on 'boy footballers' in the *Bolton Evening News*. It was well known that Wolves had a reputation for developing young players, as had Bolton, and that Ted Vizard was a vehement supporter of this policy. 'Some clubs interest themselves in boys of 14 or 15, while others regard them as young at 17 to 19. A boy grows quickly between 14 and 17, and anything can happen in those three vital years.' A fact to which the Bolton fans could certainly testify. 'It is surprising,' Vizard continued, 'how few schoolboy internationals reach the standard required in first-class football. There are, of course, brilliant exceptions. Often a boy is prominent because of two advantages – unusual physique or exceptional speed. Both may be negative before reaching the age of 20. Should a boy possess what is known as football sense, that is something he rarely loses.' While these comments were no doubt intended to be directed at his own teenage players they could, and would be equally applied to Nat Lofthouse, as Vizard well knew. Ted Vizard enjoyed being at Wolverhampton for, among other reasons, 'both the club and the people remind me of Bolton folk. I am looking forward to the time I shall bring my team to Burnden Park.'

Expectations were high as Cup fever gripped the town. There was an unprecedented demand for tickets to this War Cup game and Burnden Park's capacity was still restricted by the Ministry of Supply baskets stored on the terraces at the Burnden side of the ground. Half an hour before kick-off every available inch of the ground was packed tight with spectators. One army officer, finding the crush too claustrophobic, pushed his way out and demanded a refund which was refused. But it was not as if there would be any shortage of takers to replace him, including Billy Ainscow, who had failed in his own attempts to acquire a ticket. Outside the stadium black marketeers were already able to command two and a half times the face value of the tickets, something Billy was not prepared to do. One fan was even seen to turn down four times the printed price of his ticket. The paddocks were now so full that people were being allowed to jump the fences and sit on the perimeter track surrounding the pitch. Nervous police patrolled the Ministry of Supply storage area fearing that somebody might help themselves to the goods contained there.

George Hunt and Willie Moir scored the goals in a 2–1 win which was to send the team into their first major tournament final for 16 years. The jubilant crowd of almost thirty thousand went wild as they cheered the players from the pitch. It was 12 May 1945, just five days after the armistice had been signed heralding victory in Europe. Billy Ainscow was still on leave in Bolton on the official VE Day, and enjoyed the massive celebrations in the town that were being mirrored throughout the country. By midday on Sunday 13 May Whitehall and the Mall in London were already packed with a massive crowd that sent up a huge roar as Prime Minister Churchill left Downing Street for lunch with the King at Buckingham Palace. Still there had been no official statement. Three hours later, as Big Ben chimed 3 p.m., this vast congregation fell silent in order to catch every word Winston Churchill broadcast over the loudspeakers. Although Japan remained to be subdued, the war in Europe would end at midnight. 'Advance Britannia!' he proclaimed. 'Long live the cause of freedom! God save the King!' It was the signal for the release of years of pent-up feelings. Thousands upon thousands went wild with joy. At first they were shaking hands, then kissing and hugging total strangers. They were dancing, blowing whistles, throwing confetti and forming impromptu parades. A massive 'hokey-cokey' snaked around Queen Victoria's statue; crowds at the palace railings shouted, 'We want the King!' An exhilarating atmosphere that was to be further fuelled in Bolton by the build-up to their most important match since the war began.

The Cup fever that had been constantly bubbling in the town as the tournament progressed now exploded as tickets for the final went on sale. Queues began at 7.30 in the morning, nearly four hours before the box office was scheduled to open. Inevitably they rapidly sold out, and thousands of disappointed fans were turned away empty-handed. The Bolton Wanderers board appealed to the Ministry of Supply to move some of the storage baskets in order to increase the capacity on the terraces at Burnden Park. Responding to their request the government drafted in some German prisoners of war to remove some 24,700 baskets from the Burden paddock into the grandstand behind, thereby increasing the standing capacity by around 4,000.

This additional space was clearly needed. On the morning of Saturday 19 May the spectators began to gather outside the gates of Burnden Park three hours before they would be opened. By kick-off the atmosphere was electric. More than 40,000 people had managed to cram into the stadium and as the teams emerged from the tunnel the Manchester United fans, unable to contain themselves, poured on to the pitch to welcome their heroes. The *Bolton Evening News* reported that one red-hatted fan was 'pelted with all manner of missiles' for his troubles by outraged Bolton supporters. All around the ground the faithful twirled their rattles as they cheered the Wanderers on to the field. Fortunately a special enclosure had been set aside for wounded servicemen, but elsewhere in the stadium the St John Ambulance men were kept busy dealing with injuries caused by the crush of the crowd. As the players lined up and the Borough Prize Band marched off the field a small fire broke out in the stands. Quick-thinking action by officials with jugs of water narrowly averted what could have been a disaster. Amid all this frantic activity the action on the pitch began.

A hard-fought match developed with both teams finding scoring chances difficult to come by. United had the better of the early action, with the Wanderers coming back at them towards the end of the first half. Half-time saw the game still goalless but within two minutes of the restart the deadlock was broken. A Bolton corner had scarcely been gathered by United's goalkeeper Crompton when Nat Lofthouse came charging in, shoulder to shoulder, and bundled both men and the ball into the net. Nat raised his arm in celebration of the goal and the Bolton fans went wild with delight. This was to be the only goal of the game and it left the tie perfectly poised for the second leg one week later.

Although Billy Ainscow was due to return to Italy for his final spell in the army before being demobbed he was not overly concerned. It would surely be just a few weeks before he was back in Bolton for good. Once back in Italy, however, there was to be a final twist in Billy's wartime experience. With northern Italy finally coming under Allied control in his absence there had been a reorganisation of troops taking place in order to consolidate their position. As part of this readjustment Billy Ainscow, Ernie Forrest and several other members of the 53rd Field Regiment Bolton Artillery found themselves transferred into the 76th Shropshire Yeomanry and sent north to Turin.

It did not take long for Ernie to seek out the organisers of the Regimental football team and let them know that he and Billy were available to play. For their first appearance with the 76th Shropshire Yeomanry in an inter-Regimental match they had to travel over two hundred miles in the back of an army truck. In the run of play Billy attempted to fool his marker by abruptly stopping his quick run forward and stepping on the ball. For his trouble Billy was the victim of a hefty tackle from behind that left him with a broken ankle. Unable to return to his unit Billy was treated by the medical officer at the local army camp, where he was obliged to stay for two days before the CO himself made the trip from Turin to collect him. Ernie Forrest had been awaiting Billy's return in order to treat him to a few beers for his pains. Never one to refuse a drink Billy freely imbibed, until feeling a trifle over the limit he hobbled towards their sleeping quarters.

Many of the barracks in Italy were hastily built wooden structures with cubicles leading off long narrow corridors. Each cubicle could accommodate four men. The one that Billy Ainscow shared was situated at the very end of one of these corridors. On this first night back in camp Billy got up in the middle of the night to go to the toilet, just as he had done in Raikes Mill six years earlier. The plaster cast on his foot had been fitted with an iron stopper on its base. Billy banged and clattered his way down the corridor, and banged and clattered his way back to bed. This hideous din was repeated several times throughout the night, much to the annoyance of the other men in the hut. Next morning Billy awoke to see his bed surrounded by bleary-eyed squaddies under the leadership of Ernie Forrest. Before he had a chance to protest Billy was carried from the hut, still wearing his pyjamas, and taken to the unit's motor pool where a length of rubber hose was cut down and jammed over the iron. Delivered back to his bed Billy was left with the passing comment that at least he would not be keeping everyone awake the next night.

In fact Billy's broken ankle, or rather how he obtained it, became a source of amusement for his fellow soldiers. With the hostilities over the men were free to go into town most nights and Ernie Forrest for one would make sure that Billy was never left behind. If necessary the men would carry Billy from bar to bar, no doubt creating the need for more urgent nocturnal visits to the toilet. This camaraderie extended to all recreational activities, and when it was announced that there would be a Regimental trip to 'walk' up the Matterhorn Ernie Forrest insisted that Billy Ainscow, plaster cast and all, should accompany them. On the march to the base camp the Commanding Officer could not help noticing Billy Ainscow limping along with his rubber-covered plaster. As the troops paused for a rest the officer called Billy over and told him that the base camp was as far as he would be going. Despite offers of assistance from Ernie the order was for Billy to stay with the cooks and assist in the preparations for the meal the Regiment would require upon their return. It was a very disgruntled Billy Ainscow who sat down at the foot of the Matterhorn spud bashing frantically as his friends enjoyed a stroll in the mountain air.

Three days after Bolton's victory over Manchester United Jimmy Gittens was in the Regiment Office in Perugia, Italy, when his attention was caught by a telegram message from divisional HQ. A directive had been received ordering the handing in and disposal of military vehicles and artillery equipment in preparation for the unit's subsequent embarkation from Italy. There was a massive clearing-up operation to complete before a withdrawal could be effected, and Gittens's role meant that he would be heavily involved in the administration of this. Never one to miss an opportunity Jimmy Gittens interpreted this order in his own unique style. Ray Westwood would still be around for some time, especially as his phobia about flying meant that he would wait for a ship to take him back to England. So Jimmy solicited his assistance in 'disposing' of the equipment. With the exception of armour and ammunition anything that was not nailed down was sold to the locals. For the many Italians who had lost their homes and their possessions the opportunity to acquire tents, blankets and other essential supplies at bargain basement prices was too good to pass up. This highly lucrative entrepreneurial activity would keep Gittens and Westwood occupied for the remainder of their stay.

One of Stan Hanson's last duties before being sent home to England was to form part of a guard of honour for a Gurkha soldier who was to be awarded the Victoria Cross. There was a mad scramble to make him look the part. Borrowing the best bits of kit from his barrack room mates Stan finally turned out on parade like a bride in something old, something new, something borrowed, something blue.

Due to bomb damage at Old Trafford the return match against Manchester United took place at Maine Road, the ground of their neighbours, Manchester City. Bolton held a narrow one-goal lead from the first leg but Manchester United were confident that they would be able to reverse this result away from Burnden Park. As the teams lined up to be introduced to the Football League president, Mr W.C. Cuff, and await the playing of the national anthem, a one-legged man in a red shirt danced around the field as if to taunt the Bolton supporters that United could win standing on one leg. The Wanderers went straight in to the attack as the game began but it was to be United against the run of the play who scored first. Undeterred, Bolton maintained their attacking stance until Malcolm Barrass scored the equaliser that would take them into half time level but still ahead on aggregate. After an hour of tough play the crowd of 57,395 were brought to fever pitch as Manchester United scored again, Bryant putting the finishing touches to another breakaway goal. With half an hour to go the game was wide open. The aggregate score was level and the players, tiring from the frantic pace, had to go all out for the winning goal. Despite chances at both ends the game seemed destined for extra-time until the last dramatic twist in the dying moments. A powerful Nat Lofthouse header was well saved, but from the resulting corner Bolton's Dan Murphy headed goalwards and Malcolm Barrass helped the ball over the line with a back header. The referee blew the final whistle before the match could be restarted, and it was Bolton's Harry Hubbick, captain throughout the entire wartime period, who went forward to receive the Football League North Cup from Mr Cuff.

The celebrations began immediately. An open-topped motor coach transported the Bolton Wanderers party to the town for a confidently prearranged victory dinner at the Pack Horse Hotel. As the jubilant parade approached the town centre led by a coach in which the Bolton Borough Prize Band was playing loudly the crowd became more dense and the enthusiasm more marked. Such was the throng outside the hotel that despite police assistance the players had some difficulty in forcing their way through. It was a fitting end to the wartime efforts of Charles Foweraker, Walter Rowley and the Bolton Wanderers board of directors. The *Bolton Evening News,* reporting the following day, summed it up perfectly:

> The demonstrations of delight witnessed in the thronged streets in the centre of town on Saturday night when Bolton Wanderers brought home the League North Cup should serve as a reminder of the part sport has played throughout the war years in helping to keep up public morale. It should be generally appreciated how wise was the Government's resolve to encourage all forms of sport to provide the weekend relaxation of those called upon to provide the sinews of war and keep the home fires burning.
>
> The Wanderers are to be heartily congratulated on their efforts to keep the game going at Burnden Park. When war led to the suspension of normal competitions in 1939, the Wanderers had good reason to believe that they had a team capable of winning the highest honours. Several of their players, having previously joined the Territorials, were at once called into the army, and a new side had to be found and blended. The

manner in which the Cup has been won is an indication of how thoroughly that by no means easy task of rebuilding has been accomplished.

After this heady praise there was still one last match to be played before the 1944/45 season could be drawn to a close. Traditionally the winners of the Football League North Cup would have a play-off against the winners of the South Cup. Chelsea had beaten Millwall to claim that title and it was agreed that they would now host the last fixture at their home ground, Stamford Bridge. As the proceeds from the game were to go to the King George Fund for sailors it was felt that by staging the match in London they would attract a larger crowd. In fact 45,000 filled the stadium on 2 June, and as both clubs had elected to pay their own expenses the charity was well served by the event.

Chelsea were quick to take the lead and were still one goal up at half-time. Bolton were by now the masters of the fight-back, and the opening of the second half was to see them go straight for the jugular. George Hunt equalised, bravely volleying the ball past the oncoming goalkeeper who flattened George in the process. The tension was mounting as each team fought for the advantage, then to the horror of the crowd Malcolm Barrass was brought tumbling to the ground by a foul from a Chelsea defender who also handled the ball as he too took a dive. Despite loud protestations from the local supporters the referee awarded a penalty to the Wanderers. As Lol Hamlett stepped up to take it a number of irate Chelsea fans invaded the pitch and after a short scuffle snatched the ball, which they refused to give back. Probably fearing a violent backlash from the largely sporting crowd they quickly relinquished their prize. With some semblance of order restored to the stadium Hamlett converted the penalty for his team to claim the trophy and the title National Cup Champions.

That summer of 1945 was seen by the Football League Management Committee as the appropriate time to revert to pre-war arrangements. The war in the Far East was finally declared over at midnight on 13 August exactly one week after the atom bomb attack on Hiroshima. The management committee wished to return to the system of having a first, second and two regional third divisions. However, when this was put to their football club members it was met with stormy resistance. There was still a shortage of fuel, and rationing had yet to be abolished, both of which factors would make travel difficult, especially for those long journeys across virtually the entire country that would have to be made on a regular basis. There would also be the persistent problem of finding accommodation for players on overnight stays, particularly in the larger towns and cities that were yet to be rebuilt after the Blitz. In addition the demobilisation of Allied forces, while under way, was a long way from being completed. This would mean that many of the clubs' senior players would still be unavailable to them. Until all of these matters were satisfactorily resolved they felt that a return to the normal League programme was both impractical and impossible. The League competitions for the coming season would once again be organised on a regional basis. The return to a regular 42-game season would be the only concession towards getting League football back to its old self again, and the popular War Cup competition in which Bolton had been so successful during 1945 would be abolished in favour of a return to the familiar FA Cup. The actual trophy itself was still being held by the 1939 winners Portsmouth.

During one air-raid on this naval town this silver chalice had been saved from the ravages of a German bomb by the Pompey manager who took the famous trophy with him as he sat under the stairs and waited for the all clear. The FA Cup competition would, as always, begin for the First and Second division clubs at the third-round stage in January 1946. The Football Association did, however, make one concession to the League clubs by allowing all games up to the semi-final to be on a two-leg basis in order to attract much needed revenue into their coffers.

It was no surprise that many professional clubs were seriously in debt at the end of the war. At their last annual general meeting Derby County had put their indebtedness at £50,000. Several others were overdrawn or in debt to the tune of £20,000 or more. Bolton had fared better than many, largely due to the personal sacrifices made by the likes of Charles Foweraker, and some of the other board members. But they, like everyone, hoped that as the demobilisation gathered momentum football would see the same boom it had after the First World War.

A source of considerable pride to Bolton Wanderers was that their achievements of 1944/45 had been carried out without any large-scale use of the guesting system. Guest players were supposed to be used only as a last resort yet many teams were not averse to abusing the spirit of the system in an express attempt to win matches. For the two games against Manchester United and the final against Chelsea, Bolton had selected their teams from a total of twelve players, all of whom were signed to the club. Manchester had resorted to using two guests in the first leg, and four in the second, largely due to an injury crisis. Chelsea on the other hand had fielded eight guest players in their Wembley final against Millwall, and seven non-club players against Bolton in the cup winners match. Ironically, Bolton's Danny Winter guested for Chelsea in their Cup final victory at Wembley and then signed as a professional for them once he was demobbed, thereby ending his career at Burnden Park. Of course, Bolton's policy was better for the club in the long run, but many clubs, especially those in London, could not resist the temptation of drawing on that vast pool of players that would always be stationed nearby. For the forthcoming 1945/46 season the Football Association limited the permitted number of guest players to six per team per game, with a further reduction to three in November when it was expected that the vast majority of service players would have been demobilised. Against the express wishes of the London clubs no guests at all would be allowed in the restarted FA Cup competition.

Goodison Park was the venue for the first peacetime League game that Bolton Wanderers had played in for six long years. Lining up against Everton were four players who had appeared in the last peacetime game against Portsmouth on 2 September 1939 – George Taylor, Donny Howe, George Hunt and Harry Hubbick – and, incredibly, virtually all of their team-mates from that match six years ago would resume their Bolton playing careers during the 1945/46 season. The one exception of course was Harry Goslin. It was with a certain poignancy that George Taylor pulled on the number four shirt for that opening peacetime game.

For those Wartime Wanderers who had not yet returned to England there were still some fine footballing moments to be enjoyed in Italy. Ernie Forrest, still stationed with the 76th Shropshire Yeomanry in Turin, took full advantage of the situation and as Italian league football also began to return to normality he somehow managed to play several representative games for Inter Milan. Even to those demonstrative southern Europeans Ernie's incessant banter with the crowd and goal-mouth acrobatics must have seemed more than eccentric, probably the result of shellshock. Ray Westwood was now languishing in the medical tent of a transit camp near Naples. An accident with a truck jack that had slipped when he was performing a rare mechanical task had left him concussed. Having barely recovered from that injury he was then laid low with pneumonia. Six years of trying to use illness to get a ticket home and now this was the very thing that was delaying his demobilisation. But one by one the players were returning to Bolton to be demobbed. With only their demob suit and a few pounds' severance pay to show for six years of military service it was with a great sense of apprehension that they awaited news from Burnden Park. Along with all other servicemen they had received numerous government-published pamphlets on how to cope with a return to civilian life. There was information on the Resettlement Advice Office that had been established on Oxford Street in London's West End, where literally anyone was free to go for advice. No doubt there were a good many ex-servicemen who had no desire to return to their old jobs; they wanted to try something new, something that they may have learnt in the army, and this may well have been their first port of call. But the only jobs the Wartime Wanderers craved were the ones they had sacrificed in 1939. Walter Rowley kept loyal to Charles Foweraker's wishes of not forgetting the men who had volunteered to serve their country, and every one of those players was contacted by the Bolton Wanderers manager on their return to England with an offer of employment at the club.

Reunions of players with their loved ones were highly emotional experiences. May Hanson had come home from work one evening in late June to find a telegram waiting for her with the simple message from her husband, 'Arrived Southampton, see you soon'. May was so overjoyed with the news that she never went back to the aircraft factory where she had been employed throughout the war, not even to pick up her cards. Her lad was coming home safely and that was all she cared about. After two days anxiously waiting at home in her Sunday best clothes May was finally reunited with Stan on 27 June 1945. He had a month's leave before being stationed in a camp outside Leicester. These were tense times, as it was still being suggested that they may be sent to the Far East. May was not alone in thinking this would be grossly unfair as 'Stan and the 53rd had done their bit'. Thankfully, without any further overseas service, Stan was eventually demobbed in November and came home for good with a philosophy to which they both religiously adhered: 'Now we're going to really enjoy our lives, and not let anything stop us.'

Like May, Fanny Westwood had been informed by telegram of Ray's imminent arrival. Along with Alan and Ray's father, Sam, Fanny was at Brierley Hill station to greet him one dark day in autumn. It was the first time Ray had properly seen his son. While Ray and Fanny embraced on the small railway platform a smiling Sam looked on with a bewildered Alan cradled in his arms. Ray looked over and beckoned the small boy towards him. Alan was apprehensive. Despite being told about his father, the war, and his dad's famous footballing exploits the figure in front of him was somehow different from the photos Alan had been shown. The figure now standing in front of him was a stranger. Alan would not go to his father that day, and it would take many months of patient readjustment before their family life would settle down to normality.

Ray Westwood had returned on a Thursday. On the Friday a telegram had arrived at the Brierley Hill address from Walter Rowley, requesting Ray's immediate return to Bolton to resume his playing career. It did not take long for Ray to convince his manager and the team coach that despite the physical demands of the war he was fit for first-team action; 8 December 1945 saw Ray Westwood return to Bolton Wanderers for a home game against Middlesbrough. It was the final release from the shackles of army life and Ray responded to the occasion by scoring the winning goal in a 2–1 victory. For Nat Lofthouse it was a dream come true. He had been waiting for his hero's return ever since the very day he had signed apprentice papers. Now he had witnessed a Westwood goal from the best possible viewpoint, playing centre-forward to Wessie's inside left.

Life was returning to normal at international level as well. The first international game to be played against a foreign side had been against France at Wembley. The match had taken place on that same Saturday in May when Bolton had won the Football League North Cup against Manchester United. This had been followed by a series of Victory internationals between the home nations in which two Bolton Wanderers players were to feature. It is perhaps fitting that the dual experiences of footballers during the war were to be reflected in these international caps. Danny Winter, Bolton artilleryman and Dunkirk veteran, was called up twice to play for Wales, while the young Malcolm Barrass, who had quickly established a name for himself in the last War League, received his first England call in October 1945, to play against the Welsh and Danny Winter. Bolton Wanderers' status was definitely approaching the heights of Charles Foweraker's 1939 squad.

Ernie Forrest deftly swung Joyce Hazelton on to the Empress dance floor and off her feet. Being one of the last British troops out of Italy Ernie was still in uniform, on his end of service leave and waiting for that final release when he had responded to a request to go on a blind date a few weeks before Christmas. His friend from the 53rd, Tommy Cross, had met Joyce's friend Edi the week before, but she had refused a second date unless there was a companion for Joyce. Joyce's mother was something of a football follower, but not Joyce. Although she did recognise a few of the young players in the dance hall from their newspaper photographs, the man she was dancing with was a soldier.

'You dance well,' Joyce ventured.

'I learnt that doing sentry duty on the bridges in Italy at four a.m. in the morning. You had to keep moving because you didn't know which way the Germans were coming from. So it would be: one two three turn, one two three turn.' And by way of demonstration Ernie spun her through the movements, much to the amusement of a growing throng of spectators, especially when they almost bumped into Alma Foster and her boyfriend, Nat Lofthouse.

Ernie, like all the returning Wartime Wanderers, watched these younger players with a certain degree of envy. Denied six years of their football careers by the war the older players' team places and livelihoods were under threat from this new wave of talent. It was yet another challenge to the resilience that had brought them so far together. The second half of the 1945/46 season would be the acid test of their team spirit. Once again tragedy and glory would combine to test to the limit the mettle and strength of character of the Wartime Wanderers.

TEN

The Bolton artillerymen had been steadily returning to Burnden Park since the opening of the new season, in what was still just the Football League North. Both Donny Howe and Tommy Woodward had taken to the pitch in the very first match away to Everton. By December they had been joined by Jack Hurst, Stan Hanson, Albert Geldard and Ray Westwood. Charlie Hanks, Tommy Sinclair and Jack Roberts had also put in appearances on occasion, but in Jack's case it was very much at his discretion. As a consequence of the wounds he sustained in Italy Jack was still in the army at the end of 1945, convalescing at the Woolwich Military Hospital. There were times when he was summoned to play for the Wanderers and, using his army status as an excuse, took the time to visit his wife and kids in Swansea. Similarly, Ernie Forrest, who was one of the last Wartime Wanderers to be demobbed, was also to remain absent from the team until the closing stages of the season. As for the other surviving members of the original squad that volunteered in April 1939 they were all signed to a year's contract, although not exclusively as players. Just as when they signed as apprentices they would be expected to undertake all manner of menial tasks around the grounds. Their careers had come full circle, with little outward recognition for the sacrifices they had made.

Bolton Wanderers' success in both the League and the Cup during the previous two seasons had also served to improve the club's finances, and the board of directors was keen to recognise the players' roles in not only helping to bring this about, but also in creating a happier and more stable position at the club than they had experienced for some time. Consequently, in January 1946 the Wanderers' board applied to the Football League Management Committee for permission to pay benefit awards to those players who had given the requisite service. Although the League rule stipulated that a benefit up to a maximum of £650 could only be awarded to those players who had given five years' continuous service substantially with the first team it was apparent by the published list of recipients that a precedent was about to be set. The beneficiaries were to all intents and purposes the Wartime Wanderers: Jack Atkinson, Ernie Forrest, Albert Geldard, Stan Hanson, Donny Howe, Jack Hurst, Sid Jones, Jack Roberts, Tommy Sinclair, Ray Westwood, and Tommy Woodward. In addition there were five other recipients all of whom had seen either active service or been employed in reserved occupations. Harry Goslin's widow, Rebecca, had received the maximum benefit payment in 1944. This had probably only been achieved through the persistence and tenacity of Charles Foweraker who was determined that the promises he had made to the players when they volunteered for the Territorial Army should be honoured.

On the pitch the Wartime Wanderers had lost none of their magic. Their experiences on the battlefield had, if anything, bonded the unit even tighter, and the improving results reflected this. If the younger players felt excluded from this inner circle it was not by design, and indeed the exuding spirit only served to lift their own game, especially Nat Lofthouse's, whose life's ambition was being fulfilled, playing alongside his heroes. His own continuing status as the team's top scorer meant less to him than sharing a victory with Ray Westwood and the other 'true' professionals. Certainly Ray had been quick to re-establish his pulling power as he was once again the subject of front-page headlines in the *Bolton Evening News*. The gates were also increasing in direct correlation to the Wanderers' successes, especially in the FA Cup competition, in which Westwood was to excel. By the time they came to the second leg of round six Ray had scored no fewer than eight of Bolton's 13 goals in seven matches. He had returned to claim his crown, and the fans flocked loyally to the games to witness his resurgence. The depravation he and his colleagues had endured was now a thing of the past. A thrilling partnership between Westwood and Lofthouse had seen the Wanderers slaughter Liverpool 5–0 in the fourth round. Middlesbrough fell in the fifth, and in the first leg of the sixth round it was two grand goals from Westwood that gave the Wanderers a win at Stoke City. In the home leg Bolton Wanderers would only need to hold Stoke to a draw in order to secure themselves a place in the semi-final of the first proper cup tournament in seven long years.

It had been ten months since the armistice when the turnstiles opened at Burnden Park on Saturday 9 March 1946, but still the

Burnden Stand was packed with Ministry of Supply chemical bottles, severely restricting the ground's capacity. The club officials must have suspected early on that they would not be able to accommodate the demand. Since their first-round victory on the road to Wembley the number of spectators at these ties had progressively doubled from 25,000 at home to Blackburn Rovers to the 50,000 who had attended Bolton's 2–0 victory away to Stoke City. Already two hours before kick-off Manchester Road was just a seething mass of bodies. Even the trams could only just manage to inch their way forward as the fans pressed in on all sides. A *Bolton Evening News* representative recalled turning off this road towards the embankment turnstiles a few minutes after two. Within three steps he had found himself up against a solid mass of people. He had attempted to move to another entrance but before he could get away he was packed in tight. For the next hour he swayed and struggled, sweated and swore amid a cursing, laughing, roaring, mauling crowd of 10,000. An old man a yard or two ahead of him had passed out; his eyes were shut but he was being held erect by the crush. A tiny girl was plucked out of the turmoil and passed over a sea of heads as her still imprisoned mother cried out frantically, 'Go to the corner of Weston Street and wait for me.' The iron railway bridge leading to the embankment terrace from the opposite direction was also straining under the excess load. Men on the edge of these milling thousands climbed on to the roof of the groundsman's house. Others clambered over the high palisades, while still more tore down the protective sleepers and swarmed up the railway embankment outside the ground and found themselves a grandstand on the wagons and a locomotive engine shunted on to the siding.

Alma's friend Eileen Greenhalgh, née Barnett, was now out of the army and expecting her first child. She was still a Bolton supporter but particularly wanted to see this match because the famous England international, Stanley Matthews, was playing for Stoke City. Not wishing to presume on her friendship Eileen purchased a standing ticket for the terraces. Easing her way through the predominantly male crowd she sought a vantage point from which to view the match, but was already feeling claustrophobic in the midst of such a throng. Elsewhere a young Doug Hoyle, who was destined for a political career as a Labour MP, was also feeling uncomfortable in this mass of people all straining to catch that first glimpse of the players as they emerged from the tunnel beneath the Manchester Road Stand. The directors, club officials, wives and girlfriends of the players were enjoying the luxury of their seated accommodation, oblivious of the crush on the embankment. Joyce and her friend Edi were among the latest members of this privileged circle, alongside Alma Foster and Fanny Westwood, who had the young Alan playing at her feet.

Long before the opening whistle the overflow of spectators inside the ground had reached the touchlines on two sides of the pitch. The mass of bodies at the Bolton end started immediately behind the goal net and rose in a human terrace to the railway. Eileen was having difficulty breathing. She could feel the people closing in on her and she feared for the safety of her unborn child. The men around her sensed her plight and chivalrously made a path for her to squeeze through to the perimeter track. Once there she tacked on to a group of distressed people that were being consoled by a police officer. Her clothes were crumpled, her shoes and stockings scuffed with mud. Eileen had lost her enthusiasm for the game as she followed the officer who was attempting to get the group out through a small wicket gate close to the Manchester Road Stand, but it was padlocked. Just as the players stepped onto the field to a tumultuous cheer, and clatter of rattles, a spectator emerged from the crowd with a bunch of keys which he proffered to the officer.

The roar told those still trying to get into the stadium that the match had started. The swaying and jostling doubled in intensity. The old man, his eyes still shut, was carried a yard this way, two yards that way. His spectacles slid to the end of his nose and kindly, if none too gentle, hands pushed them back. Officially the turnstiles had recorded a gate of 65,419, yet the crowds outside had not abated. There must have been another 20,000 desperate to get into Burnden Park. Eileen was still disturbed by her experience when she was confronted by this other army, through which she would have to fight to escape into deserted streets.

On the advice of the police all the entrance gates had been closed one hour before the match was due to start but still the fans had tried to force an entry. In some areas they had even resorted to ripping down perimeter fencing. Unwittingly a father anxious for his own son's safety in this situation was to contribute to the disaster that was to ensue. Aware that the boy was being crushed he lifted him high above the surrounding heads and inched his way to a side gate. Like the wicket gate through which Eileen had escaped it was locked. There was no way of going back through the terraces to find another exit. Meticulously he picked the lock. The gate yielded and he was out into the side street which to his horror was crammed with even more people. Seeing this sudden opening they surged through it.

The match had begun. Despite his continuously deteriorating health Charles Foweraker had made it to his regular seat to watch the team he had created. May Hanson, who had moved back to Bolton as soon as Stan was demobbed, was also in the enclosure. Members of the Warburton family, representatives of the press, celebrities and lay people all joined in a common cause. Just as everyone remembers where they were when J.F. Kennedy was assassinated, so do the people of Bolton remember where they were on 9 March 1946.

The crush on the embankment terrace was getting worse. Those unfortunate enough to be standing on the barriers found their lungs coming under pressure as they were forced forward. Still they crowded in behind, until something had to give. With a sickening crash the barriers and a retaining wall collapsed, bodies tumbled and were immediately trampled underfoot, their cries going unheard as the human stampede continued, until the fallen were lying three and four deep. Those on the periphery soon grasped the enormity of the situation. Frantically they tried to pull the victims from beneath the torrent of feet. As others came to their aid the first crumpled, lifeless bodies were manhandled over the heads of the crowd towards the perimeter. In utter shock the police were obliged to receive these corpses and lay them on the track. Elsewhere in the stadium the fans roared in support of the game, all totally ignorant of the carnage on the embankment terrace. Nat Lofthouse was caught beside the referee as he blew up in the face of an advancing police officer. To this day Nat can clearly remember the officer's sombre words as he directed their attention to the bodies lying motionless at the edge of the pitch: 'I believe those people over there are dead.'

Unable to get word to the crowd as to what was transpiring the referee led the players from the pitch to tormenting jeers from the stands. Foweraker sensed something tragic had transpired, even though the others around him took little notice at first. Similarly those furthest from the incident should have detected something extraordinary when the police began homing in on the far terraces. Those directly below the scoreboard found themselves in a Chinese chain passing more and more bodies over their heads.

Within minutes of the players filing off the pitch it became a mass of people, wandering all over it, crowding the goal mouths, and packing the running track. There were more cheers and jeers as the mounted police pushed on to the ground with their horses and attempted to clear the crowd back to the sidelines.

The body count was rising dramatically. With insufficient space on the track the police started carrying corpses into the players' tunnel, where they were laid to rest beneath donated overcoats and jackets. Only the removal of the pitchside fencing, and the opening of the Burden Stand to allow people to share the available space with the Ministry of Supply stores, would prevent further casualties.

Even inside the players' changing-rooms they could hear the mounting discontent. The fans in the stands were growing restless. They began booing. Still there was no announcement over the Tannoy. The attempts to pass the news by word of mouth also fell on deaf ears. The senior police officer feared for a riot to add to this tragedy and so decided to call the players back on to the pitch. With reluctance the referee responded to the officer's request and briefed the team captains on the situation. Nat and his fellow players were physically sickened, and their faces ashen as they found themselves having to step over the rows of dead bodies laid out in the players' tunnel before emerging once more on to the pitch to a macabre roar of approval, which almost immediately subsided as the spectators' attention was drawn to the fevered activity in front of the embankment terraces. As other spectators, ambulancemen and police officers attempted artificial respiration on a number of victims laid out on a small area of turf around which a protective cordon of relatives and friends stood guard, the realisation that the heap of bodies outside this ring were dead slowly dawned.

Eileen was clear of the crowd now, but the surrounding silence was unnerving. She could sense something was wrong. Standing almost motionless she watched a policeman running past her towards the crowd. He responded intuitively to her unaired question: 'There's been a bad accident. Barriers collapsed, a lot of dead and injured.' There was a note of personal anxiety in his voice.

The pressure outside the ground had eased and the *Bolton Evening News* representative had been able to breathe again. He was able to turn unhindered. He and those around him walked a few unfettered steps, shrugged their sore shoulders and rubbed their tender ribs. The thousands that had been fighting to reach the turnstiles now spread themselves out over the carpark as the first limp burdens were carried from the stadium by the St John Ambulance men and the police. The relieved crowd were laughing, assuming the people had fainted from the heat, until the realisation that they were dead suddenly struck home to them the tragedy that had been unfolding inside Burnden Park.

Elsewhere throughout Bolton the word spread as if on a jungle telegraph. Charles Foweraker's wife and daughter had heard word from a bus conductor who shouted as his bus passed their front door. They had attempted to telephone the ground without success. It seemed an eternity before another bus pulled into the stop in front of their house and the conductor was able to confirm that Charles was safe.

The match was still playing as Eileen's policeman roamed frantically through the human debris. His 12-year-old son had defied him and gone to the match. As he lifted the improvised shrouds he feared the worse, expecting to see the lifeless face of his son. Then, as more and more fencing came down allowing the people to pour on to the field, he saw his boy, alive and well.

When the final whistle blew on a goalless draw, with the match having had no intermission, the word had finally penetrated to every nook and cranny of the stadium as to the enormity of the disaster. The sombre calmness was bizarrely reminiscent of a Good Friday seven years earlier, but on this occasion the tragedy was not in a premonition, it was stretched out before them. Thirty-three dead and more than 500 injured. Even when the war was at its fiercest and the Bolton regiments, including the Wanderers players, were known to have been involved in bloody battles, public anxiety was never more widespread than it was on that Saturday night. Every Bolton family, it seemed, must have been represented at Burnden Park.

The following morning a light breeze whistled through the deserted stadium. Nat emerged from the now empty tunnel. He was alone with his thoughts as he meandered through the discarded personal belongings that remained as a testimony to the previous day's disaster. Perhaps for the first time he began to realise what Ray Westwood and the other 'Wartime Wanderers' must have been through. For Nat this was his first confrontation with death, but for them it had been an almost daily occurrence for six years. Yet, when pushed on the subject they could only ever remember the football matches.

The government immediately set up an inquiry for the purposes of ascertaining and reviewing all the relevant circumstances so that the Cabinet would be able to consider whether any general measures should be taken to minimise the danger of similar tragedies occurring in the future. An inquest was opened at the Courts in the civic centre on the Monday afternoon at the same time as the Football Association officials were meeting to discuss setting up their own inquiry. Answering questions in the House of Commons a few days later the Home Secretary, Mr Chuter Ede, said that he was confident the police had taken all the steps open to them. He had made particular inquiries regarding this aspect and knew of nothing more they could have done without new legislation.

On Wednesday 13 March when Bolton Wanderers were at home to Bradford, the two teams stood in silent tribute to the victims of the Burnden disaster.

On goal average the Bolton Wanderers went through to the FA Cup semi-final, only to be beaten 2–0 by Charlton Athletic at the neutral ground of Villa Park, Birmingham. But they had finished third in the League table, their best-ever position since well before the war, and Nat was still the unrivalled top scorer, with 20 goals to Willie Moir's second-place nine. And Nat could remember every one of them.

Alma had accepted Nat's proposal of marriage, but as he was not yet 21 Nat did the expected thing and asked for his parents' consent. His father's first reaction was to ask with concern where they intended to live. Nat and Alma had already set their sights on a new house on Tonge Moor, for which the Halifax Building Society would supply them with a mortgage, hardly reassuring for Richard Lofthouse when he learnt that the repayments would have swallowed up most of his own meagre wages. But Nat was signed to play professional football for £12 a week, with a win bonus also in the offing, and the England selectors' eyes already being cast in his direction. He was a wealthy man, destined to be a football legend.

During the summer months Nat was busy preparing for his new role as a husband and homeowner, while still attending the regular training sessions. The new coach had added golf to their practice skills, partly because of the pure exercise, and partly because of the accuracy required. Ernie Forrest was one player who found the sport too dull. Certainly using a club had no place in his repertoire of movements. Instead Ernie would either kick the ball, or throwing it with all his might could match any pukka golfer's swing. But as they were expected to produce a scorecard after each round he dutifully marked each hole. By the end of the season Ernie had a handicap of 12, without ever having used a golf club.

By the time the first full season of professional football got under way in August 1946 there were still seven of the original 'Wartime Wanderers' in Bolton's First Division squad, alongside several others who were on the staff in 1939 that went on to serve their country. This was very august company for the likes of Nat Lofthouse and Lol Hamlett who were the only newcomers to appear in virtually every match that year. In their wisdom the Football League Association had published a fixture list that was identical to that of 1939/40, which was interrupted by war. Ironically Bolton Wanderers' results in the first two games were also action replays, losing away to Chelsea on 31 August, then trouncing Stoke City three days later, before facing Portsmouth for their first home match the following weekend.

This would be the first opportunity Fanny Westwood would have to see a game at Burnden Park since she and Ray had moved into their house in Ashby Street, Bolton. What was to be their very first home of their own, away from Ray's parents, was marred by a localised flu epidemic which was to affect five-year-old Alan. There had been similar incidents over the years; the worst in 1927 claimed 1,000 lives a day. Fortunately this strain was not so virulent, and modern medications enabled Alan to recover. All the same Fanny felt it best to leave him at home while she attended Burnden Park alone. Going to the match was something of a rarity for Fanny, and so she had decided to make an occasion of it. She had purchased a stylish three-piece suit in bright red with matching accessories expressly for her debut appearance at Burnden Park. Feeling very self-assured Fanny presented herself at the turnstile and felt inside the waistcoat pocket for her pass. In her excitement she had forgotten her passport to the ground. Although the ticket seller recognised her as a famous player's wife it was more than his job was worth to let her in without that all-important document. They were still prevaricating when Alma arrived in a hurry, only to find that she too was devoid of her Bolton Wanderers privilege ticket.

The ground was packed to capacity as the players prepared to go out on to the pitch. As Walter Rowley launched into his pre-match pep talk they were interrupted by a distraught ballboy bursting in with the news that Ray Westwood's wife was being refused admittance to the ground.

'They'll let my Fanny in or I'll not play,' Ray said, sitting down defiantly on the bench.

It was all Ernie could do to stop laughing. He had known Ray for a decade, and been a close friend for nearly all those years, but this was the very first time Ray had given a Christian name to his wife. For once Ernie resisted the urge to be flippant; he knew when Ray was in earnest. Instead he filed out with the other players; only Nat Lofthouse lingered.

'Your Alma's being kept out an' all,' added the ballboy for effect.

Rowley glowered at the boy who skulked off as Nat decided to take a stand, alongside his hero. 'I'll not go on either, Mr Rowley.'

'This'll not go down well with the board.'

'There've been times when I were selected to play for England and it didn't suit,' added Ray, enforcing his sincerity. 'So, I'd appreciate it if you would be good enough to escort my wife into the stand.'

Nat may have thought Ray was now going too far, but he was in it to the finish. Rowley was expressionless as he turned and left the changing-room.

There was considerable consternation among the crowd when they realised only nine Bolton players had emerged from the tunnel. Charles Foweraker was once again in his familiar seat to witness these events unfold. From the corner of his eye he glimpsed Walter Rowley enter the ground from the unexpected direction of the Great Lever Stand, accompanied by two women. Charles tracked them as they approached the directors box where they came into focus and he smiled in recognition. Sensing what had happened he turned his attention to the mouth of the tunnel in time to catch Ray Westwood and Nat Lofthouse appearing side by side. Charles had been at the club for fifty years, yet still there were instances like this that could stir his emotions. Standing before him were two of the finest players the club would ever sign.

As the teams lined up for the kick-off Ray turned to the wives enclosure and focusing on Fanny he waved. In six years of war he had hardly ever come home on leave, the number of letters he had written could be counted on one hand, intonations of affection were rare, almost non-existent, but in this one gesture Ray had expressed his true feelings, and this would stay with Fanny for ever.

ELEVEN

Not long after the 1946 FA Cup final between Charlton Athletic and Derby County the Wartime Wanderers' former army colleagues who had signed on as regulars and were still in Italy published a fitting tribute in the Army paper, *Union Jack*.

> Let Derby County bewilder. Let Charlton Athletic scintillate. Let 100,000 people roar. The team of the season will not be found at Wembley Stadium but at Burnden Park. And there can be no doubt that Bolton is that team. What other side could pack up, run away to win a war, and hurry back to take a leading part in the Cup battle as Bolton did? Long after the Cup Final of 1946 is forgotten we will remember the saga of Bolton Wanderers, the team who fought side by side with us, then came back with a bang.

It had been a costly war. In five years Britain alone had produced more than 102,000 planes, 25,000 tanks, over 35,000 guns and built better than 5,700 ships. Including those killed, missing and taken prisoner, or released on medical and other grounds, the total number who had served and were still serving in the British Forces was over 5,500,000. In addition there were close to another 17,000,000 mobilised in the auxiliary services, civil defence and industry. During the first half of 1944 the total monthly munitions output in Britain was six times what it had been at the outbreak of war. Globally some 55,000,000 people had lost their lives, roughly equivalent to the entire population of the United Kingdom.

The country and the town of Bolton slowly returned to normal. The day of the Manchester United Cup Final the lamp-posts and kerb stones were repainted in the dark municipal colours of pre-war. The exceptionally high level of women in employment during the war had resulted in seven new nurseries for working mothers being opened in the Bolton area. All the evacuated children had been returned to their families and the railway station nameplates re-hung. Only ration cards were to linger for a few years as a sober reminder of the hardships and deprivations the nation had endured.

Although all of the Wartime Wanderers had been able to return to their football careers there could be no denying that six years of fighting had taken its toll. Charlie Hanks was the first to quit the sport, and while George Catterall, Val Thompson, Billy Ithell and Sid Jones all received contracts at Burnden, probably as a concession to Charles Foweraker, none of them was to appear again in the first team.

Billy Ainscow finally got his chance to play at Burnden Park, but not as a Bolton Wanderer. On his demob in early 1946 Billy entered the building trade, and resumed his amateur football career playing for St Thomas Halliwell, before becoming the founder of the Harwood Youth Club team which was to win the Sunday League Cup in a final played at Burnden Park in 1948. Billy continued to be an active player until his early fifties.

The war had denied Albert Geldard his best years, and despite his many appearances in the 1945/46 season he was to turn out for only nine games in the following year before retiring from the sport.

Danny Winter, who had been with the Wartime Wanderers in Dunkirk, was not posted to either the Middle East or Italy with the Regiment. On leaving the army it was to be a source of disappointment to the Bolton fans that he never returned to Burnden Park, having chosen to sign for Chelsea instead.

Jack Hurst was a local Bolton man who had joined the Wanderers in 1934. In those formative years he was effectively an understudy for Jack Atkinson, whose persistently fine form had denied Hurst the opportunity to shine himself. Despite having been in the 1946 side that got through to the FA Cup semi final, Jack's football career nose-dived the following year; he made only three appearances. He managed to stay in the game by accepting a move to Oldham at Bolton's insistence in February 1947, from where he was to move south four years later to play for Chelmsford City. When his playing days were over Jack, who had always been a teetotaller, acquired a public house.

Due to injuries sustained while fighting in Italy Jack Roberts had made no appearances at all until the first peacetime Football League competition of 1946/47, when he became a consistent first-team regular. A total of 151 games with Bolton Wanderers between 1946 and 1950 won for him not only the captaincy of the team but also a Welsh cap in 1949. When his days with Bolton were over he moved back to his beloved Wales where he joined Swansea, later moving to the non-league team Llanelli before taking up employment in the Swansea steel works.

Donny Howe, who had risen to the rank of Battery Sergeant Major in the army, was to spend his entire playing career at Bolton, from 1936 to 1952. His playing days over he qualified as a FA coach and was later offered the post of coaching the Bolton 'B' team, after Stan Hanson. But he had decided to quit the sport and went to work for a Bolton firm of paper merchants.

Back out of the pits after six gruelling years Harry Hubbick was pleased to be able to make football his only career, albeit a relatively short peacetime one as a player. Despite having played in virtually every match since the start of the 1945 season Harry was eventually transferred to Port Vale in 1947, and soon after to Rochdale. By 1950 he was only playing part-time for Caenarfon while also working at De Havilland in Horwich, Bolton. But wishing to stay in football Harry maintained his daytime job until he passed the FA Coach Badge in 1953, upon which he was appointed coach to Accrington Stanley. As trainer coach at Halifax Town, then Preston North End, Harry was able to fulfil his ambition and keep in the game until his retirement, residing at Bolton the entire time.

Stan and May Hanson set up home in the Farnworth district of Bolton as soon as the war was over, and remained there while Stan continued to play for the Wanderers well in to his forty-first year, notching up a total of 423 appearances with the club. In 1950 Stan was invited on the Football Association tour of Canada, his only representative honour. Just as the war years had denied Stan the chance of not only breaking, but probably still holding, the club all-time appearance record, they had also cheated him of international fame. Following a free transfer to Rhyl in 1956 Stan spent two years playing part-time while also coaching the Bolton Wanderers 'B' team. Even when Stan acquired the unusual position of sub-postmaster at the Burnden Post Office, directly opposite the Burnden Park Stadium, he and May continued their residence at Farnworth.

Nat Lofthouse's career took off immediately after the war, both with his home team and as an England international. His exemplary performance in the 1953 away match against Austria in which he scored the winning goal with a spectacular diving header that saw him connect with the goalkeeper's boot and rendered unconscious even before the ball had crossed the line, won him the epithet, 'The Lion of Vienna'. But his greatest personal triumph was leading the Bolton Wanderers to an FA Cup final victory in 1958, with yet another controversial winning goal. On that occasion he bundled both the ball and Harry Gregg, the Manchester United goalkeeper, into the net with what was then an allowable barge, but today would attract a yellow card at the very least, instead of the recognition he enjoys as a living legend, and a lifelong friend of the man on the receiving end of the tackle.

Bouts of malaria and the toll of war soon told on Ray Westwood's football career. His spectacular 1946 Cup run was to be his swansong. Before being sold to Chester in December 1947, and then Darwen in 1949 (which quite coincidentally was also to be Ernie Forrest's last port of call at the end of his playing days the following year), Ray had already solicited Jimmy Gittens's help in setting up a wet fish shop, which Ernie Forrest would help him to run. Not long after Ray's retirement from the sport in 1950 his daughter Janet was born in the midst of a flu epidemic that had hit Bolton. Concern for the unborn child's safety had made Ray and Fanny decide to sell up the fish business and move back to Brierley Hill, where they were to take over the newsagent shop beside the railway station that Ray had used so often during his football career. Ray's grandson by his daughter Janet was to become a professional footballer, playing for Bradford City at the time of this publication.

In September 1946 Ernie Forrest and another Bolton player, believed to be Malcolm Barrass, were summoned to a trial for the England squad in London. In keeping with the invitations Ray Westwood had received several times before the war it requested that they bring their own towel and soap. The FA did, however, supply the train fare. Ernie suggested that if they took the coach instead the money that they saved would buy them a few beers for the journey home. What he failed to find out was that the return coach terminated in Manchester. Arriving shortly after midnight, and spent out, there was no alternative other than to walk the twelve miles to their homes in Bolton. The following month Ernie Forrest and Joyce Hazelton were married and promptly moved in with the Westwoods. Alan was turfed out of his bed, and the house turned in to turmoil. But Fanny could not be angry with him, for whenever Ernie was around there was never a dull moment. The kids in the neighbourhood must have seen him as something of a Santa Claus. On the eve of every match Ernie would gather up their autograph books and return them the day after, duly signed by every player in the opposing teams. Exactly a month after Ernie's wedding Joyce's friend Edi was to marry Tommy Cross and hold a reception at the Dovecocker Hotel at the Darwen end of Chorley New Road, some four miles from Burnden Park. Having played a full 90 minutes in what was to be their most spectacular win of the season (5–1 against Derby County), Ernie Forrest, having missed the tram, ran the full distance to the hotel to be on time for the very liquid reception. He had lost none of his stamina.

Over the weekend of 13 September 1947 the Bolton gunners had once again to prove how rapidly they could respond to an emergency. Lieutenant Colonel Greenhalgh put out an appeal to all serving and former members of the 53rd Field Regiment and their wives to attend a ceremony at the Silverwell Street Drill Hall at 7.30 that evening. A letter announcing a very important visit from a French dignitary had failed to arrive. Having had no response the sender had despatched a telegram giving only a few hours' notice of his imminent presence.

In May 1939 when the Bolton Regiment pulled out of his home town of Lambersart, Monsieur Nuytten had discovered the Regimental drum hastily concealed beneath some straw in his barn. For the entire duration of the German occupation he had kept it hidden. Now, as the Mayor of Lambersart, he was returning it to the rightful owners. It was an historic moment for both the Regiment and the town, and the spirit that had spurred Monsieur Nuytten deserved public recognition. Under the caption, 'Fine Record of Bolton Artillery', an article that had appeared in the *Bolton Evening News* as early as 2 October 1944 aptly summed up the Regiment's achievements:

> That it has distinguished itself is clear from the award of three Military Crosses, five Military Medals and four Mentions in Despatches. Those men who have gone through the entire programme, including a batch of Bolton Wanderers, have experienced all the vicissitudes of war from headlong retreat to fierce pursuit of the enemy and endured many climatic hardships from those chilly hours on the beaches of Dunkirk to desert heat, sandstorms and flies.
>
> Between Cairo and Tobruk they knew the meaning of African heat and African rain. In Iraq they survived miserable weather. In Italy conditions have varied from blazing sunshine when they landed to bitter winter cold and snow, and they have battled through all of it with the fortitude and Spartan courage that is the stock-in-trade of an incomparable fighting force slowly but surely heading for home.

SITUATION ON THE EVENING OF 1st JUNE 1940

MILES 1   ½   0   1   2   3   MILES

British troops are shown in Red, French in Green
and German in Blue.

DUNKIRK

92 Fd Regt
Malo les Bains   16 Fd Regt
1 HAA Regt
14 A/TK Regt

Leffrinckoucke

46 DIV
2/5 Foresters   53 Fd Regt
Teteghem
                    126 B
1 E Lan R
5 Bo

Fort Mardick

Mardick

S F F

Ancien Canal de Mardick

Loon Plage   68   DIV   32 DI

Coudekerque   9 Foresters   139 Bde
                              2/5 Leicesters
Fort Vallières

Les Bes Broucks

Bergues Canal

1 Loyals

Hoymille

Spycker

Gd. Mille Brugghe   Bergues   18 DIV

Bourbourgville

9 ARMD DIV
with under command
Mot Regt 'Grossdeutschland'

XIV CORPS
(KLEIST GROUP)   61 DIV   SIXTH

FOURTH ARMY   Pitgam   Soex   Quaedypre

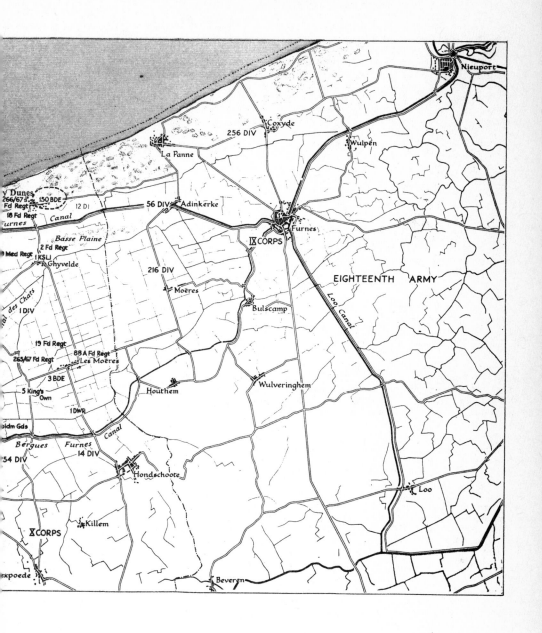

Nieuport

Coxyde

256 DIV

Wulpen

La Panne

y Dunes
266/67
Fd Regt · 150 BDE
18 Fd Regt · 12 DI

56 DIV · Adinkerke

Furnes · Canal

Basse Plaine

2 Fd Regt

Med Regt · 1 KSLI

Ghyvelde

216 DIV

Moëres

Bulscamp

Furnes

IX CORPS

EIGHTEENTH ARMY

Loo Canal

al des Chats

1 DIV

19 Fd Regt

265/67 Fd Regt · 88 A Fd Regt
Les Moëres

3 BDE

5 King's
Own

1 DWR

Houthem

Wulveringhem

oldm Gds

Bergues · Furnes Canal

54 DIV · 14 DIV

Hondschoote

Loo

Killem

X CORPS

xpoede

Beveren